SchenkerGUIDE

SchenkerGUIDE is an accessible overview of Heinrich Schenker's complex but fascinating approach to the analysis of tonal music. It builds on the widely used website www.SchenkerGUIDE.com, which has been offering straightforward explanations of Schenkerian analysis to undergraduate students since 2001.

Divided into four parts, SchenkerGUIDE offers a step-by-step method to help students tackle Schenkerian analysis:

- Part I sets out the main features of Schenker's theory and its underlying concepts.
- Part II outlines a unique and detailed working method to help students get started on the process of analysis.
- Part III puts some of these ideas into practice by exploring the basics of a Schenkerian approach to form, register, motives and dramatic structure.
- Part IV provides a series of exercises from the simple to the more sophisticated, along with hints and tips for their completion.

Tom Pankhurst is Senior Lecturer at Liverpool Hope University. His research interests include the tonal music of the twentieth century and semiotic approaches to tonality.

SchenkerGUIDE

A Brief Handbook and Website for Schenkerian Analysis

Tom Pankhurst

Liverpool Hope University, UK

Routledge
Taylor & Francis Group

NEW YORK AND LONDON

First published 2008
by Routledge
270 Madison Ave, New York, NY 10016

Simultaneously published in the UK
by Routledge
2 Park Square, Milton Park, Abingdon, Oxon OX14 4RN

Routledge is an imprint of the Taylor & Francis Group, an informa business

© 2008 Taylor & Francis

Typeset in Goudy by
Florence Production Ltd, Stoodleigh, Devon
Printed and bound in the United States of America on
acid-free paper by Edward Brothers, Inc.

Library of Congress Cataloging in Publication Data
Pankhurst, Tom.
   SchenkerGUIDE: a brief handbook and web site for Schenkerian
   analysis/Tom Pankhurst.—1st ed.
      p. cm.
   Includes bibliographical references.
   1. Schenkerian analysis.   I. Title.   II. Title: Schenker guide.
MT6.P195 2008
781.2′58—dc22   2007043058

ISBN10: 0–415–97397–X (hbk)
ISBN10: 0–415–97398–8 (pbk)
ISBN10: 0–203–92888–1 (ebk)

ISBN13: 978–0–415–97397–7 (hbk)
ISBN13: 978–0–415–97398–4 (pbk)
ISBN13: 978–0–203–92888–2 (ebk)

Contents

PART IV
Exercises   191

Visit the www.SchenkerGUIDE.com website for more exercises, a range of hints and tips, a searchable glossary plus an extensive bibliography.

Figure and examples

Figure

Examples

Preface

The basic principles of Schenkerian analysis are quite simple, but starting an analysis can nevertheless be a daunting prospect for undergraduates new to the subject. Although students can usually understand analyses and the theories behind them relatively quickly, it can often take longer to develop practical skills. The complexity of a Schenkerian analysis inevitably reflects that of the music it explores, but I have found that offering a step-by-step approach allows students to begin their own analytical work with greater confidence and accuracy.

I originally established SchenkerGUIDE.com as a quick reference tool for my students, but due to the power of internet search engines it has developed into a resource that attracts thousands of international visitors per month. This handbook has the same goal of offering a concise and accessible overview of Schenker's complex but fascinating approach to musical analysis alongside a step-by-step method for getting started.

The book is suitable for instructors who need a short and readable text to support their own pedagogy at undergraduate level or as a complement to some of the fine textbooks already on the shelves, such as Forte and Gilbert's *Introduction to Schenkerian Analysis* (Forte and Gilbert 1982) or Cadwallader and Gagné's *Analysis of Tonal Music* (Cadwallader and Gagné 1998). A detailed explanation of my suggested four-stage method lies at the heart of SchenkerGUIDE, around which I have added an overview of Schenkerian theory, some more detailed case studies and a series of graded exercises.

In order to get the most out of SchenkerGUIDE, students will need to be familiar with the basic analysis of tonal harmony with Roman numeral labels (and preferably figured bass). Some knowledge of the principles of counterpoint is advised but not presumed; while students may well not have taken species counterpoint, some experience of voice-leading through writing chorales in the style of Bach (or similar exercises) would be very helpful. Finally, some basic knowledge of Classical form is called upon in the later chapters.

This handbook is intended to be used in conjunction with the original www.SchenkerGUIDE.com website, which offers some further simple exercises, some hints and tips on presenting analyses on various music publishing packages and an extensive bibliography. It is also linked to the Routledge companion website on which can be found some further supporting materials for instructors, including powerpoints. The URL for the website is: www.routledge.com/textbooks/9780415973984.

My thanks go to David Fanning who originally suggested I produce a short guide to Schenkerian analysis for students and who has offered invaluable advice and assistance in the course of writing. The enthusiasm and occasional resistance of students in Liverpool, Manchester and Helsinki have helped to shape this book, as have the staff with whom I have worked on analysis courses and the many people who have given words of advice and encouragement on the basis of having used my website. Eero Tarasti's generous encouragement and support has also had a profound effect on my work on this project. I owe a debt of gratitude to the reviewers of this book whose comments and advice at various stages of its genesis crucially affected its final form, and to my editor, Constance Ditzel, for her excellent advice and perseverance on this project. I am also indebted to Denny Tek at Routledge, and Amanda Crook and Susan Leaper at Florence Production, for expertly guiding this book through the production process. Thanks also to Chris, Jo and Linda, who helped proofread the final draft. Finally, I am grateful for the love and support of my wife Rachael, who ultimately brought this project to fruition.

Tom Pankhurst

Part I

An overview of Schenkerian analysis

Chapter 1

An introduction to the concepts of Schenkerian analysis

Analysis, one way or another, is an integral part of musical life. On a purely practical level, sight-reading or memorizing music would be impossible if we were not able to identify simple patterns and their repetition. Our response to music as listeners is also analytical in this broad sense: we cannot help but compare melodic, rhythmic and textural ideas to those we have already heard—either in the piece at hand, or in other works with which we are familiar. The moment we move beyond an unreflective, moment-by-moment apprehension of music, whether as performers or listeners, we have entered the realm of analysis.

Up until about 1800 the description and explanation of this practical analytical understanding of music was most often found in treatises on such topics as counterpoint, figured bass, harmony, and embellishment. Analysis was, in other words, primarily a tool for explaining how to write or perform music. In the nineteenth century, however, scholars became much more interested in music of previous eras, and analysis increasingly played a part in the attempt to understand the essence of, for example, Bach or Palestrina. Most of the areas of analytical interest that developed during this period still persist today: studies of form and genre; explorations of the creative process, particularly through composers' sketchbooks; theories of harmony and counterpoint; and, finally, various attempts to describe musical works in terms of their "meaning." It is not, however, until around the turn of the twentieth century that scholars started to do the really detailed, comprehensive and systematic work characteristic of formal music analysis.

Heinrich Schenker is in many ways the high priest of twentieth-century music analysis; there are not many scholars who have managed to gain as wide an acceptance for such a novel and ambitious theory. Schenker, who was born in 1868 in Galicia (now part of Poland but then ruled by Austria), initially went to Vienna to study law but eventually enrolled at the music conservatory, where he studied, among other things, composition with Anton Bruckner. He earned his living primarily as an accompanist, teacher, and music critic, and his analytical and theoretical interests grew out of these other activities.

Schenker's writings

The most widely read of Schenker's theoretical works is *Free Composition*, the final volume of a series of books called *New Musical Theories and Fantasies*. The first in this series, published in 1906, offered a fresh perspective on harmonic theory, while the second two discussed the theory and practice of the strict (or species) counterpoint that is still taught in some universities. *Free Composition* (published in 1935) aimed to show that freely composed music was still essentially based on the principles of strict counterpoint; the way in which Schenker brings together harmonic and contrapuntal theory is one of his major contributions to music analysis. As the title of the series suggests, however, Schenker's work is as imaginative and visionary (even mystical) as it is technical. Those not familiar with Schenker sometimes caricature him as interested only in reducing music to simplistic abstract structures; it is all too easy to get this impression from *Free Composition*, which was compiled in relative haste towards the end of his life. We get a much better picture of how he puts his ideas into practice from his other two major series of analytical publications, *Der Tonwille* (which translates as something like "the will of the tone") and *The Masterwork in Music*.

Schenker focuses on the music of a fairly small number of Baroque, Classical and Romantic composers, from Bach through Beethoven to Brahms. His approach to this repertoire is encapsulated in a motto inscribed at the beginning of several of his most influential works: *Semper idem sed non eodem modo* (always the same but not in the same way). In this light, Schenker's theories can be understood as a development of the simple observation that a highly restricted set of elementary tonal building blocks (scales, triads etc.) gives rise to apparently limitless possibilities. Among other things, his analyses show how tonal compositions can be seen as the elaboration of a small number of basic patterns; it is by understanding these patterns that we can begin to identify what is distinctive about a given piece.

Heinrich Schenker's work is original and fascinating—it offers profound insights into the way tonal music works. Schenkerian analysis is, however, controversial, and those who have developed it since Schenker's death in 1935 have done so in a wide variety of different ways. In this short guide to Schenkerian analysis, I have presented its main ideas as concisely and simply as possible. I have also tried to anticipate some obvious objections to Schenker's ideas, occasionally discussing the problems and advantages of particular aspects of his approach. Analysis, like performance, is ultimately an interpretative act—it invites its readers to hear a piece of music in a particular way. Whereas Schenker lived at a time when knowledge tended to be presented as absolute truth, we tend today to view it as somewhat more provisional. The task for a student of Schenker is to be open to understanding music the way that he suggests, but at the same time keeping critical faculties intact and alert. The reward is a language for articulating musicality that no other theory offers so richly. Pursued in the right spirit, it can be a revelation.

Schenkerian analysis: some key ideas

Schenker shows that although tonal music is richly complex, it can be understood as the elaboration of simple structures that lie beneath the surface; it is this essentially simple idea of music as the art of elaboration that lies at the heart of Schenkerian analysis. Improvised embellishment has historically occupied a much more important position in classical music making than it does today. Central to realizing a keyboard accompaniment, ornamenting the vocal part of a Baroque aria, or extemporizing a virtuosic cadenza is the ability to improvize around a melody or a series of chords. In praising the "improvizatory long-range vision"[1] of the composers he particularly admired, Schenker explicitly links improvisation and composition, believing that the successful practice of both of these arts is rooted in an understanding that goes beyond the surface in order to grasp the large-scale structures of a piece of music.

In cases where there is a clearly established or pre-existing melody, the recognition of composed embellishment is an important part of the listening experience; this is the case in, for example, cantus firmus masses, Baroque arias, or virtuosic concert preludes. Schenkerian theory, however, suggests that there is always a simpler idea lurking under the surface of tonal music, even when it is not explicit in this way. The idea of music as elaboration is the starting point for the next chapter, in which the main features of Schenkerian theory are outlined. The remainder of the current chapter offers a brief informal introduction to some of the ideas that underpin Schenkerian thought.

A good analogy for the way in which Schenker suggests music works can be found in language. We process the sounds of speech by (only half-consciously) organizing them into meaningful units. No one who knows English would read or hear the following two sentences (the first two of John Steinbeck's *The Moon is Down*) as an unconnected series of vowels and consonants; understanding language involves forming relationships between its separate units:

By ten-forty-five it was all over. The town was occupied, the defenders defeated.

At the most basic level, syllables are grouped into words, but many of those words are themselves dependent on being grouped with others for their meaning. For example, the definite article at the beginning of Steinbeck's second sentence ('the') only fully makes sense when related to the noun that it precedes ('town'). An immediate analogy in tonal music can be seen in Example 1.1b, Mozart's first variation on "Ah vous dirais-je maman" (familiar to English-speaking children as "Twinkle, twinkle little star"). The neighbor notes marked with asterisks in the first measure do not make sense in the language of tonal music unless they are understood in relation to the C that they embellish; they do not make sense on their own because they do not fit with the C major harmony.

Returning to Steinbeck's opening sentences, there are points at which the prose could not be stopped without seeming incomplete (e.g. "By ten-forty-five it . . ."). The grammatical groupings that we establish as we read

Example 1.1 (a) Mozart, Variations in C ("Ah vous dirais-je maman"), K. 265, Theme; (b) Variation 1

Note: Allen Cadwallader and David Gagné offer a slightly different analysis of this passage as an example of species counterpoint in *Analysis of Tonal Music: A Schenkerian Approach* (Cadwallader and Gagné 1998: 39).

or listen to language create a continuity of expectation. If a potential group of syllables or words is left unfinished, then this continuity is broken and a tension is introduced. This works on many different levels, from the surface grammar to larger-scale meaning. Although the first sentence is grammatically complete, it nevertheless creates a tension by telling us that something was over and raising the question of what that something might be. The tension created by this incomplete information is resolved by the second sentence, in which we are informed that the subject of the first sentence is the occupation of a town. The two sentences together still leave a larger-scale tension unresolved: we wonder what will happen in the town next, and whether the defeat of the defenders is a lasting one.

There are two main underlying concepts here: first, that groups of syllables and words form meaningful units; second, that those units form tensions not only within each sentence but also from one sentence, or even paragraph, to the next. Both these ideas are important to Schenker's understanding of tonal music. In the same way that we group syllables into words, most listeners will subconsciously hear the right hand of the first measure of Example 1.1 as a group of notes organized around C. In the same way, the second measure consists of a group of neighbor notes organized around G.

Just as we moved beyond the immediate grammatical groupings of Steinbeck's opening sentences in order to explore the dynamics of the larger-scale expectations it creates, so Example 1.2 attempts to show in an informal way how we might analyze Mozart's theme (and therefore also his variation) into larger groups.

Looking first at mm. 4 to 8, I have used beams and stems to group the notes in these four measures together as a descending series of passing notes from G to C. Just as stopping midway through a sentence can produce a sense of incompleteness, so stopping after the F or the D, for example, would create a similar tension of expectation.

One reason for the sense of incompleteness may simply be knowledge of how this nursery rhyme is supposed to go. According to Schenkerian theory, however, there is a more fundamental reason why stopping after the F or

Example 1.2 "Ah vous dirais-je maman," melodic analysis

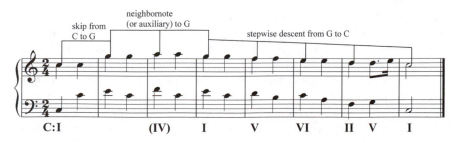

neighbornote
(or auxiliary) to G

skip from
C to G

stepwise descent from G to C

C:I   (IV)   I   V   VI   II   V   I

D has this effect. Example 1.2 is in C major, and the second part of the phrase (mm. 4–8) begins and ends on the tonic (I) of this key. The passing-note progression from G to C makes sense as a unit because it begins and ends on a tonic chord. From a Schenkerian point of view, the passing notes in between are an elaboration of this tonic harmony. If you stop on F or D the embellishment of the tonic is incomplete and this is what creates the tension that binds the notes together.

The comparison between this musical extract and my Steinbeck example is quite close in that stopping at some points creates less of a tension than others. If you break off after "The town was occupied" (leaving out "the defenders defeated") it makes grammatical sense but offers less information. A comparable musical effect might be created by stopping the second part of the phrase of Example 1.2 after the first E in m. 6: there is still a complete meaningful unit that begins and ends on the tonic chord of C even though the phrase is incomplete. The first four measures of the theme also make up a complete musical unit: first a leap from C to G and then an upper neighbor note to that G. Again, finishing on the neighbor note in m. 3 would create a tension, a sense of incompleteness.

One final analogy can be drawn between linguistic and musical structures. I have already suggested that Steinbeck's first sentence sets up a tension that is then resolved by the sentence that follows. The way in which *musical* tensions are set up and resolved is very different, but the first four measures of Example 1.2 likewise introduce a tension that is resolved in the eighth. Schenker suggests that melodies that do not finish on the first degree of the scale (the tonic note) sound less final or closed than ones that do (an idea we shall return to later). He argues that finishing on any other degree of the scale will prevent the sense of complete closure. If this is true, the second half of Example 1.2 sounds closed because it ends on scale degree 1 (C) but the first half of the tune (up to the G on the first beat of m. 4) does not. In that case, the lack of complete closure in the first half creates a tension that is resolved in the second. The analogy of the tension of expectation followed by resolution is rather looser, but the principle is not so very different.

Schenker extends this insight in his later work to show how the sort of structure shown in Example 1.2 spans whole movements and pieces, and this sort of insight is what makes Schenker's work both fascinating and problematic: fascinating, because his analyses offer a way of discussing otherwise elusive notions about the shape and direction of phrases; problematic, because there is a tendency to ignore other factors such as rhythm, texture and dynamics.

It is easy to see why top-rank musicians such as the pianist Murray Perahia and the conductor Wilhelm Furtwängler have found Schenker's ideas attractive. Players and conductors are often concerned about the long-term shape of the pieces they play, and Schenkerian analysis offers a way of analyzing this aspect of music. It is equally easy to understand why others have been hostile to an analytical technique that seems to rely on simplifying musical works in order to expose less interesting underlying patterns. You will doubtless encounter arguments both for and against Schenkerian analysis, the value of which you can assess for yourself, but it is important to make your judgment on two separate but related criteria: first, whether Schenkerian analysis successfully addresses the questions it asks; and, second, whether those questions are worth asking in the first place.

Chapter 2

An overview of the basics

Music and elaboration

Schenker understands music as an art of elaboration, a point of view that is easiest to appreciate in a theme and variations, as we saw in the previous chapter. Example 2.1 shows the beginning of Beethoven's variations on "God save the King" (or "My Country, 'Tis of Thee"). Starting at the top (Example 2.1a), Beethoven's first variation on this theme adds a number of embellishments, some of which are labeled.

In the first measure of Example 2.1a, Beethoven decorates the melody with a neighbor (or auxiliary) note, which adds an unaccented B in between the first two C naturals of the original theme. A similar figure can be seen at the beginning of the third measure. The appoggiatura at the end of the same measure is more striking: Beethoven leaps to an accented G that descends onto the F that it elaborates. The arpeggiation at the end of the second measure is, on the other hand, a relatively discreet embellishment in which the melody leaps from the original D natural to a note from the same chord (G major) before continuing.

It is possible to understand a theme and variation as two layers: the theme (Example 2.1b) is a simpler layer on top of which the embellishments of the variation (Example 2.1a) are built. One of Schenker's most important ideas is that even the most complex tonal music is layered in this way; the relationship between a theme and variation is not a special case but a particularly clear example of a more general principle.

This general principle can be seen by comparing the theme in Example 2.1b with the Example 2.1c, which is a simplification of this melody. The theme's various embellishments can be understood as being built on top of the simplified version in Example 2.1c. The basic method of Schenkerian analysis is to understand tonal music as the embellishment of hypothetical layers beneath the surface. A dissonant note such as the first E of m. 5 of the theme, for example, can easily be identified as an appoggiatura embellishment of the following D. In the simplified version of the melody in Example 2.1c, the embellishing E is therefore omitted. As it happens, the original

Example 2.1 Beethoven, Seven Variations on the National Song "God save the King" (or "My Country, 'Tis of Thee"): (a) Variation 1; (b) Theme; (c) and (d) Analytic reductions

melody of "God Save the King" does not include the E either—Beethoven has begun to elaborate his theme before he has even started the variations.

Not all analytical decisions, however, are just a matter of identifying dissonant notes. In the first measure of the theme, for example, although neither C nor D are dissonant, the D is identified as a neighbor note. One important factor in coming to the decision that D embellishes the C (rather than the other way around) is that the most structurally significant harmony in m. 1 is the C major tonic (I) with which it starts. In looking for an underlying melody it therefore makes sense to focus on the C, as D is not part of this main harmony (as well as being rhythmically less prominent).

This analytical decision produces the lone C in the first measure of Example 2.2c—the D on the final beat (along with its associated harmonic support of II) is omitted from the simplified theme because it is understood as an elaboration. This does not, however, mean that D is less important than C any more than the variation is less important than the theme; the aim of this sort of analysis is to explore the basic structure of the music.

The neighbor note in the third measure of the theme may also be understood as an elaboration of the more prominent and harmonically significant E, but the second, fourth and fifth measures introduce another form of embellishment. In m. 2, the B and D are connected by a passing note C that is dissonant with the main dominant (V) harmony; like the neighbor note in the previous measure, this embellishment is therefore omitted in the Example 2.1c. A Schenkerian analysis, however, aims to show the simplest possible structures upon which the elaborations of music are based, and because B and D are both part of the same dominant harmony, it is possible to boil down m. 2 even further, as shown in Example 2.1d. The rationale behind representing this measure as a D rather than a B is explored in detail in both this and later chapters, but one of the reasons for this decision is that the D makes a smoother and simpler connection between the first and third measures than B, which would involve a leap of a fourth up to the E in m. 3.

Whereas "God save the King" is demonstrably the starting point for Beethoven's set of variations, the further simplifications of Examples 2.2c and 2.2d are only hypothetical. What they reveal, however, is the underlying shape of this well known melody, which turns out to be an arch from C to E to C. A Schenkerian analysis aims to imagine the complexities of tonal music as elaborations of simpler layers beneath the surface of the music. Just as a harmonic or formal analysis deepens our knowledge, so delving beneath the surface of a piece of music in this way ultimately increases our understanding both of its larger-scale shape and its intricate details.

Compound melody

Melodic embellishment is often discussed in relation to a single melody—in the previous example, the top voice of the piano texture. However, a melodic line can also suggest several voices, as shown in the extracts below from one of Bach's violin partitas; these intricate solo works, like the cello suites, are able to conjure up a melody, a bass line and sometimes several inner parts. A single melodic line that implies several voices in this way is known as a compound melody.

At the opening of this Chaconne, Bach asks the solo violin to triple stop in order to produce three simultaneous voices. In the bracketed section of Example 2.2a, however, although the violin is now only double stopping (two notes at the same time) the music implies the three voices shown on the lower staff. Bach achieves this effect in the last measure by skipping between the two upper voices in sixteenth notes instead of playing them simultaneously. At the end of the previous measure, Bach decorates a skip between the G and E of the upper two voices with passing notes.

Later on in the Chaconne, the violin plays a more complicated compound melody, in which a single melodic line of sixteenth notes suggests several voices as shown in Example 2.2b. Here the relationship between the figuration and the notional three or four voices is a little less straightforward, but no less important for that—the two measures shown clearly outline a chordal progression from II to V to I in G minor.

Just as the embellishment that is typical of variations turns out to be an important feature of music in general, the implication of several voices in Bach's solo string music demonstrates a musical principle that is found in a wide range of circumstances. The Alberti bass in the left hand of Example 2.3 offers an example of a basic compound melody in a piano piece by Mozart. This single line of sixteenth notes can be simplified, as shown in Example 2.3b, into a series of triads. Understood from this point of view, the Alberti bass skips between the three implied voices of a much simpler chorale-like texture.

The right hand of Example 2.3 works in a similar way to the left hand in that it moves between notes from the same two triads; the way in which it does so, however, is much freer. In the first two beats, the melody leaps up from B♭ to D, but from there a turn and two passing notes (E♭ and E) connect to a downwards leap from F to C. Whereas the left hand gives more or less equal prominence to the three implied voices, the right hand emphasizes some notes more than others.

Example 2.2 J. S. Bach, Partita No. 2 in D minor for Violin Solo, BWV 1004, Chaconne: (a) Mm. 1–3; (b) Mm. 42–3

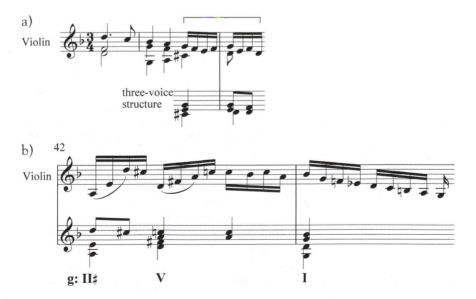

Anyone who has tried to write four-part chordal textures in the manner of a Bach chorale will be familiar with the concept of *voice-leading*. Voice-leading is the way in which the different voices of a multi-part texture behave, both on their own and in relation to each other. The voice-leading of the bass staff of Example 2.3b is very simple: the top voice (F) stays on the same note, while the lower two voices move down by step in parallel thirds. Educators have developed various guidelines for voice-leading in Bach chorales and other styles, which include avoiding parallel fifths between two voices and recommendations on the balance of steps and leaps within a single voice. These voice-leading principles, which are of considerable importance to Schenkerian analysis, are further discussed later in this chapter.

Example 2.3 Mozart, Piano Sonata in F major, KV 332, Adagio

The idea that tonal music can be understood as the embellishment of chords is very important to Schenkerian analysis—the various melodic and accompanying figures of these few measures of Mozart breathe life into the simple harmonic progression from I to V. However, Schenker's real achievement was to show how tonal music is generated not only as an embellishment of harmonies but also as the development of small and large-scale linear patterns. A Schenkerian analyst would be interested not only in the sequence of chords shown in Example 2.3b (the vertical dimension), but also in the linear patterns found in the voice-leading (the horizontal dimension).

At the core of Schenker's approach is an adaptation and synthesis of traditional ways of understanding the horizontal aspect of music (counterpoint) and the vertical aspect (harmony). Although Schenker makes some robust criticisms of traditional harmonic theory, the basics of this aspect of his analytical method will be reasonably familiar to most students. His approach to counterpoint, however, draws on a particular method for teaching students to write counterpoint, which might be somewhat less familiar. The practicalities of these harmonic and contrapuntal ideas, so central to Schenkerian thought, are briefly discussed below.

Harmony and figured bass

We shall see later in this book that Schenker's ideas on large-scale harmony are quite radical; the practicalities of the basic harmonic labeling that Schenkerians use, however, will be familiar enough. The system used in this book involves a standard combination of Roman numerals and figured bass.

Example 2.4 gives some examples of Roman numerals and figured bass in practice. A letter followed by a colon denotes the relevant key, with minor keys in lower case; Roman numerals (all in upper case) indicate the chord within that key. At its simplest, the addition of figured bass to the Roman

---

Figured bass is a shorthand method of indicating harmonies that was widely used in the Baroque era to allow keyboardists (and other continuo players) to improvise an accompanying part above a given bass line. Arabic numbers written beneath the staff indicate what intervals above the bass note should be played. Figured bass is commonly used by analysts to show details of harmony and voice-leading.

The only real complication is that the full figuring (i.e. figures for all the intervals above the bass) is abbreviated in order to avoid cluttering the score. Therefore, if no numbers are written, a continuo player will presume that they are to play a fifth and a third above the bass—a root position triad (see example). The number 6 below the staff tells the player to keep the third but replace the fifth with a sixth above the bass, forming a first inversion triad. A second inversion triad is indicated by telling the player to replace the fifth and third of the default root position chord with a sixth and fourth above the bass. As well as indicating triads and sevenths in their various inversions, figured bass is also used to show suspensions within a chord, such as 4 resolving to 3, as in the last measure below.

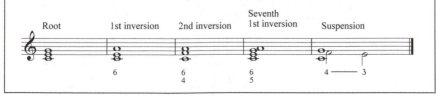

numeral labeling system can be used to clarify inversions, as in the first chord of Example 2.4a, where the 6 below the staff (short for 6/3) shows that the dominant chord is in first inversion. The real advantage of figured bass, however, is that it is a very efficient way of labeling some of the most common embellishments of chords. A good example is the last chord of the cadence in Example 2.4a, which is decorated by a suspension. The figuring 4–3 shows that this E♭ major triad is decorated by a suspended fourth (A♭) that resolves to the third (G) on the second beat.

Example 2.4 (a) (b) and (c) Mozart, *The London Sketchbook*, KV 15, No. 28; (d) *Eight Minuets*, KV 315, No. 8

a)

b)

c)

d)

Example 2.4b shows another embellishment commonly found at cadences. In the last measure of this extract, the same 4–3 figure appears as a decoration of V, but instead of being suspended against the fifth of the chord it is accompanied in parallel thirds 6/4–5/3. Some traditional harmonic labeling systems would label the first chord of m. 49 as a second inversion of chord I (i.e. IC). Although this is not actually untrue, such figures are much better understood as a sort of appoggiatura onto the final chord rather than two independent harmonies. It is the same principle as in the previous example, in which the suspended fourth was understood as part of a linear embellishment of the chord rather than a chord in its own right. The second inversion chord I here is a linear embellishment of chord V, and the figured bass labeling shows this clearly.

The 6/4–5/3 pattern seen in Example 2.4b is a very common figure and is often referred to as a *cadential six-four*. Whereas in Example 2.4b it decorates an arrival on V (a half close or imperfect cadence), cadential six-fours are even more common as part of a perfect cadence, as shown in Example 2.4c. Again, while a traditional analysis might label the second beat of m. 59 as a second inversion of chord I, it is shown here as an approach to, or decoration of, the dominant. Although not every second inversion chord is only a decoration of another harmony, Example 2.4d shows how even a long series of six-fours can still be understood as linear embellishment. As we will see in the course of this chapter, this linear approach to understanding the functions of music is an important part of Schenkerian thought.

Counterpoint

The harmonic element of Schenkerian analysis strongly relies on traditional functional harmony, even though Schenker disagreed with some of its main theoretical conclusions. The linear or contrapuntal element of his ideas also grows out of traditional practice, in this case a long-established method of teaching students about counterpoint. This method prescribes a series of highly restrictive exercises based on the style of high renaissance composers such as Palestrina. The practice of dividing such exercises into a number of different "species" (or types) of counterpoint has a long history that goes back to the middle of the sixteenth century. "Species counterpoint" formed part of the musical education of such major figures as Haydn, Mozart,

---

Take the time to play through these examples on the piano—you will find that everything in this book makes much more sense if you do so. Failing that, you will find midi files of many of the examples on www.SchenkerGUIDE.com.

Beethoven and Brahms; the principles it embodies are integral to the compositional tradition to which these composers belong.

Starting at the bottom of Example 2.5, a student of species counterpoint is given a simple tune called a cantus firmus, above (or below) which an increasingly elaborate melody is added in counterpoint. In first species, for example, the new line must move in rhythmic unison with the cantus firmus. In second species the added voice instead consists of two notes for every note of the cantus firmus, and in third species, four notes per note. The fourth species involves adding a syncopated line while the fifth is a relatively free combination of all the previous species plus some extra embellishments. Having worked on two-part exercises in all five species the student then moves to three-part counterpoint.

It is easy to see the general relevance of species counterpoint to Schenkerian analysis by comparing, for example, the fourth and fifth species in Example 2.5; the notion that a simple melody can underpin a more complex one is very clearly demonstrated by the way in which the fifth species decorates the suspensions of the fourth. There are, however, three main ideas from species counterpoint that are particularly important to Schenkerian analysis: first, the principles of voice-leading (i.e. the recommendation against particular types of motion between voices, such as parallel fifths); second, the control of dissonant intervals, which can only appear in tightly restricted circumstances as elaborations of consonant ones (i.e. a passing note moves by step between two consonant notes); third, the concept of what Schenker calls "melodic fluency," which describes the way in which Palestrina's polyphony tends to keep different types of melodic motion in balance and

Example 2.5 An example of species counterpoint

proportion (there is a preference for stepwise motion and leaps are usually balanced steps in the opposite direction). Schenker's suggestion is that the principles of voice-leading, dissonance treatment and melodic fluency underpin tonal music both on the smallest and the largest scale. The importance of species counterpoint to Schenker is demonstrated by his two-volume book on the subject, in which he demonstrates how its principles are masterfully extended in the work of the composers he most admires; he also points out how they are ignored by those he scorns.

Most tonal music does not immediately resemble the very restricted progressions allowed in first and second species counterpoint, but Schenker suggests that underneath the surface embellishments the basic structure of Baroque and Classical music is governed by the same principles. He shows how the counterpoint seen in Example 2.5 provides the framework around which even highly complex musical textures are based. A very simple example of this can be seen in Example 2.6, in which a Mozart orchestral score can be understood as an elaboration of what could easily be first species counterpoint. Schenker develops this basic idea in his analytical work, eventually showing how whole movements can be understood as elaborations of such simple contrapuntal frameworks.

Analytical layers

Schenker's notion of music as contrapuntal elaboration adds a new dimension to the analysis of music: that of depth. This can be observed on a rudimentary

Example 2.6 Mozart, Symphony in G minor, K. 550, first movement

level in species counterpoint; Example 2.7 re-organizes Example 2.5 to make this clear. Although each species is self-sufficient, the more complex fourth and fifth can be understood as elaborations of the first. Schenkerian theory uses the metaphor of layers to describe these relationships. The more complex "surface" of the fifth species could theoretically be stripped away to reveal the simpler fourth species below, which in turn could be simplified to reveal the first species exercise. To turn it the other way around, one can understand Example 2.7 as documenting a move from the deepest (and simplest) layer of first species to the surface elaborations of the fifth. In this particular case, each of these layers is a self-contained exercise, but Schenkerian theory suggests that a hypothetical journey from simplicity to complexity, from depth to surface, can be traced in the composition of tonal music and in the way in which we understand it.

You might suppose that Schenkerian analysis therefore involves a mechanical process of reduction: the surface of the music is stripped back to reveal the simpler layers underneath. Although it is of course true that we can only start with the surface of the music and, from there, construct the deeper analytical layers, the actual process of analysis is more subtle and complex.

The main reason for this is that a Schenkerian analyst looks at the surface and asks not "which notes should I strip away?" but "how can I understand this surface as an elaboration of the patterns and structures that Schenkerian theory proposes?" Schenker suggests, for example, that the deeper levels of a piece of music embody many of the principles of species counterpoint (e.g. avoiding parallels, preferring stepwise motion). In addition, he outlines a

Example 2.7 Species counterpoint as a series of layers

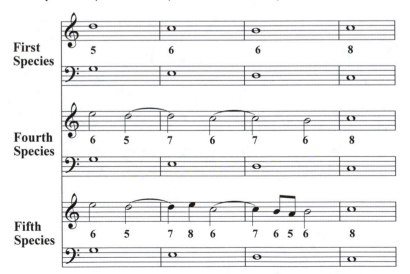

Foreground, middleground and background

Schenker gives formal labels to the various layers of an analysis. The analysis of the surface of the music is called the *foreground*; this first layer of analytical work is concerned with the complex details of the music as it appears on the page. At the other end of the scale, the simplest and deepest layer of the music is called the *background*. Whereas the foreground may be infinitely varied, Schenker suggests that the background will conform to one of a fairly small number of contrapuntal structures. A background graph, which represents a whole piece or movement, can contain as few as three notes in an upper voice counterpointed against the same number of notes in the bass.

Depending on the length and complexity of the piece, an analysis will consist of a varying number of layers in between that explain how the foreground relates to the background. These *middleground* layers increase in complexity and detail as one moves towards the foreground. The middleground layer closest to the background is referred to as the *first-level middleground*, and consists only of direct elaborations of the background.

---

fairly restricted number of basic contrapuntal structures that underpin tonal music and the main ways in which they are elaborated. The process of analysis therefore involves trying to work out how the surface of the music can be understood as elaborations of these basic contrapuntal structures; this means a constant shuttling back and forth between surface and deep layers, trying out different solutions until a satisfactory one is reached. Although this process is quite complicated, the basic principles that underpin it are actually quite simple. In Chapter 4 I offer a methodology for getting started on this analytical process, while most of the rest of the present chapter is devoted to explaining the main principles and structures involved.

Basic melodic elaborations

Schenker calls the process of elaboration from one analytical layer to another *prolongation*. Harmonies, which are essentially static, become activated by their contrapuntal embellishment; at the same time, complex embellishments are intelligible only through their relationship to the harmonies that they elaborate. At its simplest level, Schenkerian analysis is therefore the search for contrapuntal embellishments of harmonies.

Figure 2.1 shows the main basic categories of melodic elaborations, dividing them into consonant and dissonant. On the left-hand side of the table the

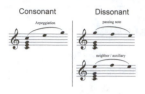

Figure 2.1 Basic melodic elaborations

arpeggiation skips between notes from the harmony it prolongs (in this case C major), while, on the right-hand side, there are dissonant elaborations of the harmony notes, involving stepwise motion (i.e. major or minor seconds). The next part of this chapter is devoted to explaining these basic melodic embellishments and showing some examples of them in action. It is important that there is always a clear relationship between the melodic elaborations and the harmonies that they elaborate.

Arpeggiation

An arpeggiation is a series of skips between the notes of a single chord in the same direction. Example 2.8a shows some examples of arpeggiations and also introduces the basic notation of foreground melodic elaborations: the notes of the arpeggiation are represented with stemless note heads and grouped together with a slur; a Roman numeral below the stave indicates the harmony that is being elaborated.

In the first measure of this example the upper voice ascends through the three notes of a root position triad against a lower voice that sustains the

Example 2.8 Arpeggiations of C major

a)

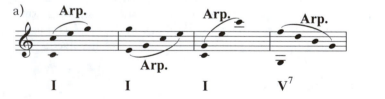

b)

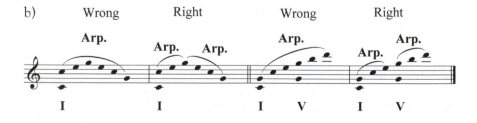

Notice that the fourth arpeggiation in Example 2.8a contains a seventh (F in a chord of G). Sevenths are usually considered a dissonant interval, but the dominant seventh chord is such an important sonority in tonal music that most analysts consider the seventh as a sort of honorary consonance in this context. Most seventh chords (particularly those involving a major seventh) are considered too dissonant to be treated in this way, but another exception is the diminished seventh chord. As the diminished seventh is effectively a stack of minor thirds, it contains no dissonances and can therefore be arpeggiated.

root note of the chord, elaborating the harmony of I in C major. There is quite a lot of freedom as to what constitutes arpeggiations: they can begin and end on any note (see m. 2 of Example 2.8a); they can also miss notes out (see m. 3); and they can appear in any voice. However, there are two important conditions that define an arpeggiation: first, it can only elaborate one chord; second, it can only skip in one direction. As shown in Example 2.8b, if a series of skips changes direction, or if the harmony changes, then in Schenkerian terms more than one melodic elaboration is involved. It is very important to avoid the mistakes demonstrated in Example 2.8b: in the first measure two arpeggiations (one in each direction) are wrongly grouped under one slur; in the third measure a string of notes is grouped together that implies a nonsensical harmony—such bitonality (I and V) has no place in the tonal language with which Schenkerian analysis is concerned.

The final movement of Beethoven's Op. 27, No. 2 Piano Sonata "Moonlight" (Example 2.9) offers a clear example of arpeggiations in different layers of the musical texture. The slurs in the right hand in the first two measures suggest that we hear the continuous surface of the music broken up by the changes of direction before the beginning of each arpeggiated octave (G♯ to G♯ in the first group of four sixteenths, C♯ to C♯ in the second etc.).

Beneath this busy surface it is possible to pick out a series of slower arpeggiations that each span two measures in the middleground. There are three immediate reasons why the choice of notes marked with stems and beams in Example 2.9 seems intuitively persuasive: first, these notes are melodically prominent as the highest note of each foreground arpeggiation; second, they coincide with the underlying quarter-note pulse; third, they constitute a two-octave arpeggiation in their own right (e.g. from G♯ at the beginning of m. 1 to the same note at the end m. 2).

One of the criticisms sometimes leveled at Schenkerian analysis is that it reduces the foreground to a skeleton middleground that has little bearing

Example 2.9 Beethoven, Piano Sonata in C♯ minor, Op. 27, No. 2 ("Moonlight"), Presto agitato

on the listening experience. Example 2.9 is a good counter example in this regard because the fast tempo of this extract means that the middleground two-measure arpeggiations are actually easier to hear than the blur of sixteenth-note foreground arpeggiations. The analysis shows how the music divides into melodically and harmonically unified two-measure units, a division that one might well make intuitively, but Schenkerian analysis provides a formal method and notation for analyzing the shape and dynamics of the phrases in these terms.

Schenker uses the word *Brechung* (meaning 'breaking' as in broken chords) to describe arpeggiations.[1] A skip between just two notes is not generally considered an arpeggiation because it is often better understood as a movement between the two voices of a compound melody. Example 2.10a is a good example of this situation. In m. 1, the violin in the upper staff plays a series of two-note arpeggiations of chord I in D minor; after each set of two notes the melody changes direction, so the notes have to be split up into pairs in this way. As with the examples of compound melody above, the eighth notes can be simplified to show a two-voice texture as shown in the upper staff of Example 2.10a. Both the upper and lower voices of this simplified version can be understood as three-note descending arpeggiations, marked with slurs on the example. The crotchets in the bass part are also similarly simplified into two-note chords, and the whole pattern is repeated in the next measure but this time elaborating chord V.

Example 2.10 Corelli, Violin Sonata, Op. 5, No. 12, Adagio

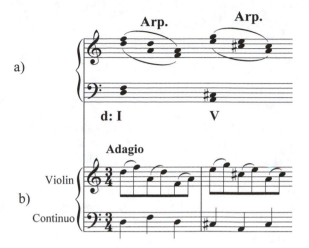

> Notice that a Schenkerian analysis does not attempt to notate duration. Example 2.10a shows the succession of notes without indicating how long each one lasts. The rhythmic notation and articulation is stripped away in order that the same symbols can instead be used to communicate the analysis, in this case the grouping of these pitches into arpeggiations.

Neighbor notes

A neighbor note (*Nebennote* in German) is related by step to the note that it elaborates and is usually dissonant with the underlying harmony. A complete neighbor note moves away from the harmony note and then returns, whereas an incomplete neighbor is missing either the first or last instance of the harmony note. Examples 2.11a and b are therefore complete neighbor notes—the dissonant note lies between two statements of the same harmony note (C). Example 2.11c, on the other hand, is an incomplete upper neighbor note. In Example 2.11d an upper (D) and a lower (B) neighbor note make a sort of pincer movement onto the harmony note (C)—this figure is sometimes called a double neighbor note.

Neighbor notes are a familiar enough surface elaboration; indeed, almost the whole of the second prelude from Bach's *The Well-Tempered Clavier* is animated by neighbor-note elaborations. Example 2.12 shows the first measure of this C minor prelude. In the first beat, C and E♭ are both members of the prevailing harmony of chord I in C minor. The D, however, is not

Example 2.11 Neighbor notes prolonging a C major harmony

part of this chord—it is an embellishment of the E♭, from which it moves by step before a return to the harmony note.

Example 2.12 is also a further example of a compound melody. Without the neighbor notes, the right hand simply skips between the notes of the tonic harmony, creating the three-voice chord shown in the upper staff. The left hand similarly decorates a compound melody, this time with lower neighbor notes (the F naturals are neighbor notes to the G).

If the neighbor notes in the Bach are very much a foreground (surface) phenomenon, in Example 2.13 they play a more important role in shaping a short passage from a Schubert Impromptu. As shown in Example 2.13, the right hand skips between two voices in the first couple of measures; both voices form complete neighbor-note elaborations—an upper neighbor in the top voice and a lower neighbor in the bottom. Whereas the compound melody in the Bach was decorated by neighbor notes, here two voices created by the compound melody form a pair of neighbor notes.

Even in this short example, one can see the complex relationship between harmony and counterpoint in Schenkerian theory. The E♭ and the A are elaborations of D and B♭ respectively and, as such, can be understood from a purely contrapuntal point of view. On the other hand, these notes can

Example 2.12 J. S. Bach, *The Well Tempered Clavier*, Book 1, Preludio II

Example 2.13 Schubert, *Six Impromptus*, Op. 142, No. 3

As with all the examples from this point onwards, the deeper analytical layer is presented at the top with the music below. Schenkerian analysts present their graphs in this way because they are more interested in how the music can be understood to be generated from the deepest layer than in the process of reduction.

be understood as part of a harmonic progression from tonic to dominant and back. The neighbor-note figures form a thread that unifies this short passage into a contrapuntal realization of the tonic of B♭ major. Because the E♭ and A are dissonant in relation to the main tonic harmony, they create a tension that is resolved only when the neighbor-note figure is complete. One of the interesting things about Schenkerian analysis is the way in which such patterns of tension and resolution can be projected across increasingly larger spans of music.

Linear progressions

A linear progression (*Zug*) involves stepwise motion in one direction between two harmony notes. A simple illustration can be seen in Example 2.14a, in which a passing note progression spans a third: the D connects C and E in order to create an ascending linear progression. Such a progression is referred to as a third progression (3-prg) because it spans the interval of a third.

Example 2.14 Linear progressions prolonging a C major harmony

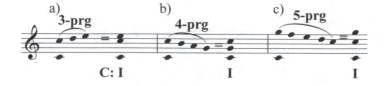

Most linear progressions are best understood as the elaboration of a leap between notes that belong to different voices within a single chord. Example 2.14a is therefore a movement from a lower voice (C) to a higher voice (E) within the same C major harmony. The two realms of harmony and counterpoint are thus interdependent: harmony is animated by melody but a melody can only make sense in tonal music through its relationship to underlying harmony.

Example 2.14b is analyzed according to the same principle: the first and last notes are consonant with the harmony (C major) and the resulting two-note chord is fleshed out by a motion from the upper voice (C) to the lower voice (G). The linear progression therefore creates a coherent unit; the two dissonances (B and A) span the gap, creating a thread of continuity across all four notes. Example 2.14c is similarly an elaboration of a two-note chord involving C and G, this time spanning the interval of a fifth.

Linear progressions play a central part in Schenkerian analysis because they allow us to show how passages of music of various lengths are elaborations of the sort of stepwise motion favored in species counterpoint; they provide a unifying thread around which complex surface embellishments can be woven.

A simple example of linear progressions in the foreground can be seen in Example 2.15. The basic harmony of chord I in G major remains the same throughout these four measures, and it is elaborated by a rising third progression followed by a falling fourth. Notice how Example 2.15a does not show the incessantly repeating G naturals in the bass—consecutively repeated notes are usually omitted in order to reduce clutter on the analysis. In this example, I have also left out the inner voice in the right hand; it is normally a good idea to retain inner parts in a foreground analysis but I have omitted them here for the sake of clarity.

In Example 2.15 the passing notes are dissonant and as a result they cannot easily be further elaborated. One key feature of linear progressions as we move deeper beneath the surface of the music is that passing notes have their own harmonic support in the foreground and can therefore be embellished. Example 2.16 provides an abstract illustration of this process. The deepest layer (Example 2.16a) shows a D passing note that is dissonant with the C major tonic harmony it prolongs. In Example 2.16b, however,

The harmonic sense of linear progressions is vital to Schenkerian theory, and one of the most common mistakes made by students is to join together conjunct notes without thinking carefully about the harmony that these progressions suggest. Part (a) of the example below shows an analytical mistake of this kind. The upper slur marks out a fourth progression from C to F, while the lower slur marks out a progression from E down to B. The harmonic implications of these two fourth progressions are incompatible: C and F suggest an F harmony while E and B suggest an E major or minor chord. Part (b) suggests an analysis of the same pitches that does make harmonic sense: the two third progressions both imply the chord of C major. The F in the top part and B in the lower part are explained instead as neighbor notes.

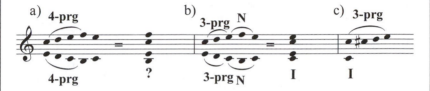

Part (c) demonstrates a common misunderstanding. The term "third progression" refers to the interval spanned by the progression rather than the number of notes it contains. This rising sequence of notes spans a third from C to E and is therefore not a fourth progression. The C♯ is, in fact, an extra chromatic passing note between the C and the D and does not affect the harmonic sense of the progression.

Example 2.15 Mozart, Piano Sonata in G major, KV 283, Presto

Example 2.16 Decorated third progression

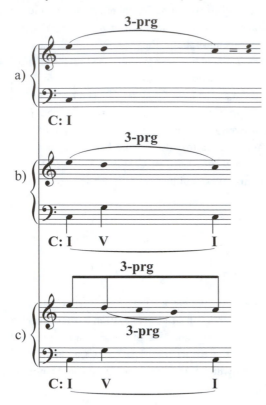

Hierarchical notation

The notation in Example 2.16c shows how the third progression from D is subordinate to (or less structurally important than) the overall descending third progression from E that it decorates. More structurally important notes are marked with stems and beams, and their embellishments are shown by unstemmed note heads that are connected to them with a slur. Schenkerian notation in this way sets up a hierarchy of relative structural importance. This does not of course imply that notes lower down the hierarchy are less musically important; it simply means that they embellish notes that lie "deeper" beneath the surface of the music. Whereas the third progression from E spans the whole of Example 2.16 and is therefore the deepest level of the example, the progression from D is a decoration closer to the surface.

the D is given support in the bass by G (suggesting a dominant harmony), which allows it in Example 2.16c to be further elaborated by its own third progression. Schenkerian analysis seeks to understand music in this way, imagining how the surface (Example 2.16c) arises from hypothetical simpler layers beneath it.

Example 2.17 shows a third progression at the beginning of a Mozart theme and variations. To look at this music from a Schenkerian perspective, you need to start at the top and imagine the passage developing from its simple origins, like a plant growing from a seed. Example 2.17a shows the initial descending third progression over chord I in E♭ major, in which the A♭ passing note is dissonant with the E♭ major harmony. The first stage of growth

Example 2.17 Mozart, Variations in E♭, KV 353, Thema

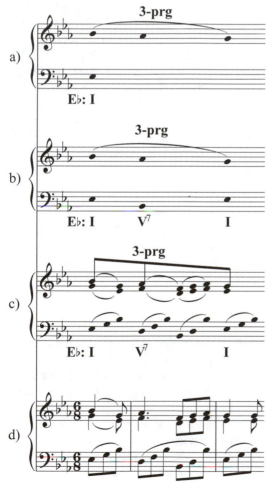

is shown in Example 2.17b where this passing note is supported by chord V as a dominant seventh. The harmonic support for this passing note makes it possible for it to grow further, as in Example 2.17c, in which we can see the Ab decorated by its own rising third progression. Example 2.17c also shows the various other elaborations that arise at the surface of the music, including the shadowing of the entire top line in thirds by a lower voice and the arpeggiations in the bass. From a Schenkerian point of view, this passage is therefore understood as the elaboration of the deeper level descending third progression shown in Example 2.17a. This simple structure is both harmonic (in that it elaborates chord I in Eb) and contrapuntal (in that it involves two voices working in counterpoint). It has the potential to be elaborated in an almost infinite number of different ways.

Example 2.18 offers a final example of a linear progression in practice, this time as a decoration of another elaboration deeper still beneath the surface of the music. Starting again at the deepest layer, Example 2.18a shows an E over the main harmony of I in C major, which is elaborated by a neighbor note (D) over the dominant. Example 2.18b introduces a rising third progression to this initial E in which the passing note is supported by V. The third progression is subordinate to the underlying neighbor note but, as shown in Example 2.18c, it has its own embellishing neighbor notes on the surface of the music.

This example offers a flavor of the complex relationships involved in even a very short passage of music. Schenkerian analysis aims to explore these relationships and show the simple structures that underpin such surface complexity.

Further elaborations

The three main types of elaboration (arpeggiation, neighbor note and linear progression), along with the concepts of compound melody and musical layers, form the foundations of Schenkerian analysis. Everything outlined in the rest of this chapter and the next builds upon and refines these concepts.

Unfolding

As outlined in the discussion of compound melody, a single line can imply more than one voice. A common type of elaboration is for a melody to skip back and forth between two implied voices, a device Schenker calls unfolding (*Ausfaltung*). The right hand of the piano part in m. 51 of Example 2.19 descends in parallel thirds. The first measure of the extract is similar but instead of presenting the thirds as two simultaneous voices, the sixteenth notes skip from one to the other in alternation. The two-note chords (a vertical phenomenon) are unfolded horizontally into pairs. A similar unfolding in dotted rhythms can be seen ascending in m. 52.

Example 2.18 Mozart, *Eleven Minuets*, KV 176, No. 1

Unfoldings are not always so easy to spot, because they do not necessarily only unfold neat pairs of thirds or sixths. As always with a Schenkerian analysis, Example 2.20 (the beginning of a Beethoven piano sonata) is best read starting on the top staff, which represents the deepest level, and working down to the actual music in Example 2.20c. The top staff of Example 2.20a shows the two-voice structure that is implied by the music—the upper voice stays on B♭ while the inner voice moves down by step. As shown in Example 2.20b, the two chords are in opposite directions as the melody first skips down a third and then up a fourth. Because the unfoldings are in

Example 2.19 Haydn, Piano Sonata in E♭ major, Hob. XVI, No. 28, Allegro moderato, mm. 49–54

> Some analysts discuss such two-note skips in slightly different terms, notably Forte and Gilbert, who distinguish between embellishments that proceed up or down a complete triad (an arpeggiation) and those that skip from one note of the chord to any other (a consonant skip).[2] You may well come across this terminology, and it can sometimes be useful, but most consonant skips are better understood in terms of compound melody as unfoldings.

different directions, the first and last notes of the melody form the upper voice (B♭) while the second and third form the lower.

There are various ways to notate unfolding, but the beams and stems in Example 2.20b are the most formal method of doing so. The upward stem on the first note shows that this is the upper voice and the downward stem on the second indicates that it is from the lower voice. The two notes of the unfolding are connected by additional opposing stems connected by a diagonal beam. The second unfolding is presented in the same way but the opposite way round.

In Examples 2.19 and 2.20, the melody skips between two voices with no interruption, an unadorned type of unfolding appearing in the foreground, right on the surface of the music. Example 2.21 shows a middleground unfolding that is decorated in various ways on the surface and is therefore slightly harder to spot. Example 2.21a shows the three-voice structure implied by the music: the bass holds down a tonic pedal; the top voice consists of a rising and falling third progression; the middle voice doubles the pedal before filling in some harmonies towards the end.

Example 2.20 Beethoven, Sonata quasi una fantasia, Op. 27, No. 1, Andante

A simple foreground unfolding such as Example 2.20 can be notated more simply to avoid cluttering up the score. The upper voice is marked with an upward stem and the two are connected either by a slur or a diagonal line, in which case a downward stem can be added to the lower note. In more complex middleground unfoldings (such as the next example) the more formal notation is much clearer.

The top staff of Example 2.21b shows how these two upper voices are unfolded and embellished. The first interval of the third is unfolded with an upwards skip, which is followed by a descending unfolding from Ab to Eb. Whereas the first unfolding is unembellished, the second is filled in with passing notes. Unfoldings quite often work in this way in conjunction with

Example 2.21 Haydn, Piano Sonata in E♭ major, Hob. XVI, No. 52, Moderato

other types of elaboration. It might seem easier just to label this as a descending fourth progression, but understanding it as a progression that fills in an unfolding exposes the underlying two-voice structure, which in turn uncovers the rising and falling third beneath the surface of the music. The next unfolding is filled in with an ascending arpeggiation, whereas the final interval of a sixth is not unfolded at all. The foreground therefore involves a number of different types of elaboration, but they are ultimately held together by the underlying two-voice structure shown in Example 2.21a. The basic shape of this passage is exposed by Example 2.21a as an arch, a simple rising and falling. As we shall see, Schenker's ambition was to reveal underlying shapes of this kind over a much larger scale. Penetrating beneath the immediate surface detail is an important skill to which instrumental teachers frequently appeal when they ask students to consider the longer-term shape and direction of a musical line. Schenker himself was a piano teacher and, to some extent, his analyses can be seen as an attempt to formalize this type of long-range musical thinking.

Additional points

Where the slightly more complex pieces of music being explored in this section throw up issues that are not immediately relevant to the topic under discussion, these questions will be addressed briefly outside the main text. There are a few such issues that arise out of Example 2.21:

1   We have already encountered passing six-four harmonies and this is another good example. The A♭ passing note is harmonized by a six-four harmony that we might otherwise label as chord IV in its second inversion. The subdominant quality of this chord is emphasized by the D♭ in the second beat of the m. 1, which briefly makes the tonic sound like a dominant seventh approach to A♭. Without the pedal this could be a true subdominant harmony; the dominant that follows is constrained in the same way, but there is no sensible way of figuring this.

2   The two third progressions appear to go against the principle set out above that they are movement between two voices in the same harmony. Here the B♭ is harmonized by V rather than the main tonic harmony. As discussed below, it is quite common for the beginning and end of linear progressions to be harmonized by the dominant in this way—the move to and from V in this passage reinforces rather than weakens the overall sense of the tonic.

3   The inner voices are omitted in Example 2.21b in order to avoid an analysis that is too cluttered to read easily. Inner voices should not be left out of analyses lightly, but here there is more to be gained by the clarity that their omission brings than there is from leaving them in.

Some refinements to linear progressions

Linear progressions connecting two harmonies

The linear progressions discussed so far fill the gap between two notes from the same harmony; in certain circumstances, however, linear progressions can move between two notes from different harmonies. The harmonic sense of elaborations is crucial in Schenkerian theory, so a linear progression of this type must make sense of the goal harmony—the chord that supports its final note. This is the case in the third progression analyzed in the second part of Example 2.22. The D is supported by chord II, while the B is harmonized by chord V. The B and D are both notes from the dominant, so the progression makes sense of the harmony at its goal.

Example 2.22 Haydn, Piano Sonata in C major, Hob. XVI, No. 15, Air

There is, however, an exception even to this general rule, demonstrated in the fourth progression with which Example 2.22 opens. Sometimes, the last note of a linear progression that starts on the tonic is harmonized by the dominant. In this case, the C and G are both members of the tonic harmony, but the arrival on G is marked by a change of harmony to the dominant. A move from tonic to dominant in the course of a linear progression, as in this example, is the only exception to the above principle that a linear progression must make sense of the harmony at its goal. The reason for this exception is that the relationship between tonic and dominant is such a strong one that the overall harmonic sense of the progression can still be understood.

Dominant sevenths

I have so far defined a linear progression as a stepwise motion between notes that are consonant with the relevant harmony. One grey area, however, is the dominant seventh, which we have already encountered in relation to arpeggiations. Schenker offers somewhat contradictory advice in this area, but there are plenty of examples in which he shows dominant sevenths being elaborated. In their text book on Schenkerian analysis, Allen Cadwallader and David Gagné define such cases as secondary linear progressions, acknowledging that they exist but that they have a different (and less stable) nature compared to ordinary linear progressions.[3]

Example 2.23 shows two slightly different cases. In m. 25 (the fourth of the extract) a linear progression of a seventh elaborates the dominant seventh chord. The second measure could be read in a similar way as a linear progression of an octave, but one might also argue that the eighth notes simply transfer the seventh at the beginning of the measure down an octave—

Example 2.23 Beethoven, Piano Sonata in C minor, Op. 13, Rondo, mm. 23–7

the A♭ could, in other words, be interpreted as a highly elaborated passing note between the B♭ at the end of the previous measure and the G at the beginning of the next. Such surface decorations are obviously of a different order from proper linear progressions, which can span much larger distances.

Leading progressions

Many of the examples have concentrated on the outer voices (melody and bass) of musical textures, but it is important not to forget the way in which linear progressions in the inner voices can interact with these. Sometimes, as in Example 2.24a, two voices in parallel thirds or sixths are both "true" linear progressions, in that they pass between notes that belong to the harmony (in this case C major). Sometimes, however, one of the voices does not make sense from a Schenkerian point of view, in that it does not seem to elaborate the relevant harmony. This is the case in Example 2.24b, where the lower of the two voices passes between C, which is part of the tonic harmony, and A, which is not. In such cases, Schenker suggests that the voice that does prolong the harmony is structural but that the other merely adds some texture by shadowing this main voice. Here, the top voice is said to be the "leading progression" while the other voice shadows it in "lower thirds."

Example 2.24 Lower thirds

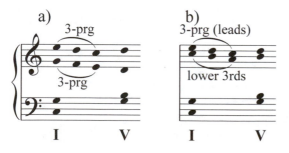

The beginning of the Haydn piano sonata shown in Example 2.25 offers an example of a leading progression. The main descending sixth progression in the upper voice moves from the tonic in the first measure to the dominant at the end of the second, conforming to the principle outlined above that the first and last notes of a linear progression must make sense in terms of the harmony at its goal (G and B natural are both part of chord V). The inner voice in the second measure, however, does not make any harmonic sense on its own—it cannot be a fifth progression from A to D because this does not fit with the dominant harmony. One rather convoluted solution would be to treat the initial A as a neighbor note leading onto a descending fourth progression from G down to D, but it is much simpler to understand it as shadowing the upper voice in "lower sixths."

Before moving on, it is worth looking at a final example that brings together some of the features encountered so far. As already noted, Schenkerian analyses are best read starting from the deepest layer in order to see how the music can be understood as an elaboration of a simple structure; an analyst, however, must of course begin with the score. In the following example, therefore, I will take a slightly more practical approach, working from the surface and moving towards the deeper layers of the music. The focus remains on introducing the basic elements and concepts of Schenker's theory rather than on a working method for analysis, which is outlined in Chapter 4.

Example 2.26c is a foreground analysis of the opening of the trio from Beethoven's first piano sonata. The process of foreground analysis is to show how each chord is elaborated by combinations of arpeggiations, neighbor notes and linear progressions. The initial tonic of the first measure, for

Example 2.25 Haydn, Piano Sonata in C minor, Hob. XVI, No. 20, Allegro moderato

example, is decorated in the right hand by a rising skip (a foreground unfolding), followed by a neighbor note embellishment of A and finally an ascending third progression from F to A. In the left hand the elaboration is by means of a rising arpeggiation. The second measure follows a similar pattern, and most of the remainder of the passage is equally straightforward in the foreground. One of the few minor complications is that the descending linear progression at the end of m. 2 is an example of a linear progression that connects two harmonies rather than moving between two notes of the same harmony. In connecting II and V it fulfills the conditions of such a progression because its first and last notes (G and E) are both notes from the goal harmony of V. The descending third progression at the end of m. 3 in the right hand is a similar case, connecting V and I.

A Schenkerian analysis seeks to move beneath the surface to uncover the underlying progressions, and in Example 2.26 this is achieved in two stages.

Example 2.26 Beethoven, Piano Sonata in F minor, Op. 2, No. 1, Trio

Additional points

Two further points arise out of this passage:

1   The arpeggiations in the left hand can also be interpreted as a compound melody consisting of three implied voices as shown in Example 2.26a. This suggests a slightly different interpretation of the left hand of m. 2, in which it skips between the notes of a last inversion chord II (figured 4/2 on the example). If this seems to make rather too much of the seventh chord on the last beat, it does have the advantage of simplifying the bass line to a neighbor note elaboration F–E–F.
2   The first unfolding from C up to A implies a leap from an additional voice below the main unfolding. Although it is quite common for melodies to leap to or from an inner voice that is not exploited in the rest of a passage, this particular C can be understood to be continued in the top voice of the compound melody implied by the bass part.

The first (Example 2.26b) suggests that the foreground neighbor notes and third progressions in the first two measures of right hand are elaborations of descending unfoldings, skipping between an upper and a lower voice as shown by the stems and beams. Once these have been folded back up into a pair of parallel rising thirds (as shown in Example 2.26a) the upper voice links through to the C in m. 3 to create an underlying ascending third progression. This provides another example of the only exception to the rule that the first and last notes of a linear progression must at least fit with the harmony at its goal, namely when the harmony moves from tonic to dominant. The A at the beginning and C in m. 3 do not fit with V but they do with the initial I. The analysis therefore understands the series of eighth notes on the surface as the embellishment of a rising and falling third progression, revealing the basic shape of the passage. As we shall see in the next chapter, this process of looking beneath the surface can be continued much further beneath the surface to reveal longer-term shapes and patterns across much larger spans of music.

Linear intervallic patterns

We saw in the Mozart extract in Example 2.6 how a complex surface was the elaboration of a note-against-note counterpoint. In the Mozart, this counterpoint consisted of a chain of parallel sixths, a very simple example of a linear intervallic pattern—the repetition of an interval or series of intervals. A slightly more complex pattern that occurs very frequently is alternating fifths and sixths, as seen in Example 2.27. The lower two parts of this extract describe a series of thirds, but the upper part moves on the second and fourth beats of the measure and creates the alternating pattern with the bass.

As a harmonic progression, this passage is rather odd, with rising root position chords (V–VI–VII etc.) on the strong beats interleaved with a series of first inversions on the weak beats (III6–IV6 etc.); it makes more sense to understand it in terms of the main linear intervallic pattern of 5–6–5–6. As shown in Example 2.27c, this does not mean that we cannot explain this Corelli extract in terms of the ideas outlined so far in this chapter: the underlying dominant harmony is realized by a rising fourth progression in the top part counterpointed against a rising third progression in the bass. The linear intervallic pattern simply explains how the upper and lower voices interact contrapuntally.

Example 2.28, another extract from a Corelli violin sonata, shows a slightly more complex linear intervallic pattern. Although there are only two parts, the violin plays a compound melody, skipping between two upper voices as shown in Example 2.28b. The resulting three-voice counterpoint (reminiscent of third species) interlocks a series of seventh suspensions that each resolves onto a tenth with the bass (7–10–7–10). It is very common for linear

Example 2.27 Corelli, Violin Sonata, Op. 5, No. 3, Allegro

Schenker discusses 5–6 linear intervallic patterns at some length as part of his exploration of how the principles of species counterpoint underpin tonal music. He sees 5–6 patterns as one of a range of strategies that composers use to avoid parallel fifths, which are forbidden in strict counterpoint. Without the interpolated sixths, this rising series of root position chords would blatantly violate this rule.

intervallic patterns to be associated with melodic sequences, as in this example, in which the two parts repeat a pattern descending.

As in Example 2.27, the underlying contrapuntal structure of the passage can be understood as a linear progression (a descending sixth in the top voice from C down to E as the elaboration of a C major harmony), but the notion of linear intervallic patterns helps explain in simple terms what would otherwise seem a rather complex elaboration of this idea.

Example 2.28 Corelli, Violin Sonata, Op. 5, No. 4, Adagio

Reaching over

Example 2.29 shows a short passage from a Mozart Andante in which the principal form of elaboration is arpeggiation: in the right hand each measure ends with a rising arpeggiation while the left hand skips between three voices in an Alberti-style compound melody. Despite the simplicity of this extract, the relationship between the arpeggiations in the right hand and the notes on the strong beat of each measure raises an interesting question.

Example 2.29c, below the main example, suggests interpreting the passage as a series of unfoldings: the C at the beginning of the first measure unfolds up to the top of the arpeggiation (E) with the same pattern of a rising unfolding third being repeated in the second measure. The underlying elaboration in the top voice in this analysis is therefore the neighbor note E–F–E. This is a logical solution based on the analytical tools introduced so far, but it is not a musically intuitive one for two reasons: first, it privileges

Example 2.29 Mozart, *Nannerl's Notebook*, KV 6, No. 2, Andante, mm. 9–11

the last sixteenth note of each measure over the much more heavily empha-sized pair of eighth notes at the beginning of the measure; second, it does not reflect the fact that the arpeggiations at the end of each measure feel like they lead onto the beginning of the next. Play through this extract on the piano to see if you agree that this interpretation is unsatisfactory.

Example 2.29d offers an alternative solution, interpreting the passage in terms of what Schenker calls reaching over (*Uebergreifen*). Rather than understanding the E at the end of the first measure as an upper voice, this analysis shows it "reaching over" an underlying third progression in order to drop down onto the D. This reading reflects much better the sense that the end of each measure leads onto the next main accented beat.

A reaching over therefore has two elements: first, it involves leaping up above the main voice; second, it must descend by step onto the note being elaborated. It nearly always involves a rising linear progression or arpeggiation being decorated by a descending incomplete neighbor note or third progres-sion. The subject of the second A-major fugue from Bach's *The Well Tempered Clavier* (Example 2.30) offers a more compact example of the same pattern. After an initial flurry of sixteenths, each step of a rising fifth progression is preceded by a reaching over of a third in order to drop by step onto the main voice. As in the last example, it is not easy to make good sense of this passage by treating this series of thirds as unfoldings.

As well as elaborating rising linear progressions, the reaching over is also found in conjunction with rising arpeggiations. Example 2.31 shows an example of this in which the melody leaps up in order to descend stepwise onto the second and third notes of an arpeggiation of F♯ minor. Unlike in previous examples, the first reaching over introduces a new harmony—a diminished seventh chord on E♯ that resolves onto a return to the original tonic note. The second reaching over is a little more complex because, in anticipating the E♯ at the end of the first quarter of m. 17, the melody also incorporates an unfolding. The F♯ at the beginning of the measure is, as shown in the figuring, a suspension onto the E♯. Schenkerian analysts employ eighth note flags for a number of different purposes on their graphs, sometimes

Example 2.30 J. S. Bach, *The Well Tempered Clavier*, Book 2, Fugue XIX, mm. 5–6

Example 2.31 Chopin, Mazurka in G# minor, Op. 33, No. 1, mm. 16–17

simply to draw attention to particular notes but often to show a reaching over, as in this example.

Schenker proposes two basic models of reaching over: in the first the reaching over introduces an elaborated note by descending to it by step (as in all the above examples); in the second the elaborated note is itself the reaching over. This is the case in the fifth progression shown in Example 2.32, which is decorated by a series of lower neighbor notes. Each note of the fifth progression is regained by reaching over the lower neighbors. This type of reaching over is less common than the first, but Example 2.33 shows a figure that is frequently encountered in which the first type is followed by the second, resulting in a double neighbor note embellishment first of B and then of D.

Example 2.32 Haydn, Piano Sonata in G minor, Hob. XVI, No. 44, Allegretto, mm. 25–8

Example 2.33 Haydn, Piano Sonata in C major, Hob. XVI, No. 50, Allegro, m. 34

G: I

Voice exchange

The rising fifth progression shown in Example 2.34a is unadorned except for the F, which is elaborated by a pair of third progressions in contrary motion in the upper and lower voices. These linear progressions in the second full measure are a decoration of a simpler underlying procedure, which Schenker calls a voice exchange. The F in the top line, as shown by the diagonal line, swaps with the F in the bass while the A in the bass is swapped into the upper voice; we therefore end up with the two voices exchanging pitches. In this example, the upper part unfolds the interval of a third from F to A, but because the bass does the opposite at the same time (unfolding A to F), the whole figure can be understood as an exchange. As a voice exchange is a special type of unfolding, it is frequently found in conjunction with other types of elaborations such as the third progressions found in this example.

Example 2.34 Mozart, *Twelve Minuets*, KV 103, No. 1

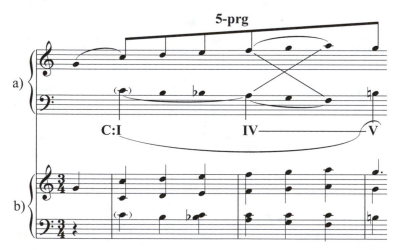

As we have seen in this chapter, Schenkerian analysis involves under-standing complex surfaces in terms of underlying patterns. The analytical graphs are read from the deepest level through to the surface, so that we can trace the imagined "growth" of the piece from its simplest origin to its fully developed form. It is like looking at a plant and trying to imagine how it developed stage by stage from its seed.

In practice, however, we have to begin our analysis at the surface of the music. This is assisted by the relatively small number of elaborations that Schenker suggests we are likely to find (arpeggiations, linear progressions, neighbor notes and their various combinations). The process of analysis, outlined in Chapter 4, therefore involves moving backwards and forwards between the layers as we try to see what the simplest way of understanding the music is going to be. As we move from the foreground deeper into the background structure we shall see that Schenker offers us a great deal of help in this process by suggesting some common patterns on which long passages and eventually whole pieces are usually based. It is these larger-scale basic patterns and their elaborations that are outlined in the next chapter.

Chapter 3

Larger-scale structures

The chorale phrase shown in Example 3.1d might seem a strange starting point for a chapter on larger-scale structures; despite its brevity it nevertheless demonstrates some of the main features of Schenker's approach. This is possible because the deepest layers of tonal structure according to Schenkerian theory are extremely simple; it is in the elaborations of these structures that complexity arises. Example 3.1 shows how this phrase elaborates a G major chord both contrapuntally and harmonically. Conceptualizing it from the deepest level to the surface, the tonic chord (a) is elaborated by a third progression (b), to which is added a contrapuntal line in the bass (c). This basic two-part counterpoint is then fleshed out with inner parts to become a fully harmonized chorale phrase (d). This phrase therefore grows out of the tonic chord of G major, both contrapuntally and harmonically.

Schenker proposes a number of basic patterns that are found most frequently in the deep background structure of tonal works. These models share two main characteristics of the chorale phrase in Example 3.1: the overall harmonic shape of I–V–I and the descending linear progression in the upper voice. The simple journey from tonic to dominant and back to tonic is one found in virtually all tonal pieces, and Schenker's suggested structures all elaborate this basic scheme in some way. Example 3.1 provides a clear

Example 3.1 Chorale phrase

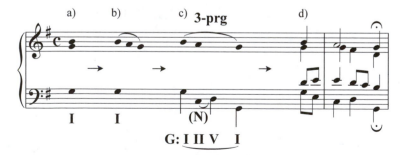

Although the upper voice patterns of Schenker's proposed background structures and their immediate elaborations move largely in stepwise motion (we shall encounter these elaborations later in this chapter), the bass part tends to contain a greater number of leaps. This is because the bass line is not only a contrapuntal voice but also harmonic support for the texture, which means that root position and first inversion chords predominate. The tendency for the bass to leap more than the melody is a feature of conventional tonal voice leading that is particularly clear in Bach's chorales.

(if very brief) illustration of how a bass part might elaborate a I–V–I structure. The root of the dominant chord (D) is decorated in a way that can be understood both as a melodic elaboration (the C is a neighbor note) and as a harmonic elaboration (II as preparation for V).

Bass prolongations

Schenker suggests that the harmonic pattern of I–V–I seen in Example 3.1 is common to all tonal music. This reflects the facts that virtually all tonal pieces begin and end in the tonic and that they almost invariably close with a move from dominant to tonic (most obviously the final perfect cadence). As most of the action of a piece therefore occurs between the initial tonic and the final dominant of this model, it could be represented as follows (X stands for the intervening harmonies):

I–(X)–V–I

Schenker proposes a number of standard ways in which this I–(X)–V–I structure tends to be elaborated in the tonal repertoire, and a few of these are outlined in Example 3.2. One of the simplest ways of elaborating the motion from I to V is through an arpeggiation, as shown in Example 3.2b, with Example 3.2c demonstrating a further elaboration of this pattern, in which the resulting gaps are filled in to make a series of passing notes.

Example 3.2 Examples of I–V–I structures

Bass terminology

Schenker calls the bass part of his background structures the *Bassbrechung*—the "breaking" of the bass. The span in the bass from I–V can be "broken" in a number of ways, of which Example 3.2 shows only a few. All the *Bassbrechung* structures above from a) to d) employ what Schenker calls a *third-divider*. The third-divider bisects the span from I–V by dividing it at the third into a rising arpeggiation.

Example 3.2d shows a minor key variant of the Example 3.2b. Here the middle of the arpeggiation (the E♭) is not harmonized as a first inversion tonic, but as chord III, which is preceded by its own dominant (B♭).

Finally, Example 3.2e shows another common basic pattern in which the dominant is approached not though the third but by a lower neighbor note that represents the harmony of IV. *Bassbrechung* is quite often translated as "Bass Arpeggiation." This is slightly misleading, because we would normally expect an arpeggiation to move through the consonant notes of a particular harmony. As suggested by Example 3.2e, the arpeggiation is only one of many possible *Bassbrechung* patterns.

The bass patterns shown in Example 3.2 form the deep background of tonal pieces; their ultimate elaboration in the foreground might span hundreds of measures of music. Schenker calls the main harmonies represented in these diagrams *scale-steps* (*Stufen*)—they are more structurally important than ordinary harmonies because they represent the basic harmonic pillars of the piece. The surrounding harmonies are less important in that they are part of a linear-harmonic elaboration of these pillars or scale-steps.

Elaborations of the bass

The concept of the *Bassbrechung* is difficult to grasp in the abstract, so it is worth illustrating how it can be elaborated in a number of short extracts. Although these structures can often be found on a relatively small scale as in the examples below, it should be remembered that the *Bassbrechung* is principally a background structure that spans complete movements.

A very simple prolongation of the *Bassbrechung* shown in Example 3.2c can be seen in the extract from a Haydn piano sonata shown in Example 3.3. This passage illustrates quite clearly the notion of scale-steps. The main harmonies are those of the *Bassbrechung*, while those in brackets are passing harmonies that arise primarily out of the contrapuntal elaboration of this basic structure. The main function of the eighth notes at the end of the first two measures is as passing notes rather than as independent harmonies.

Example 3.3 Haydn, Piano Sonata in G major, Hob. XVI, No. 11, Presto

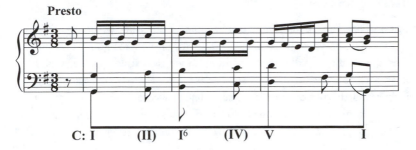

Example 3.4 shows a more complex bass prolongation based on the pattern from Example 3.2d. The bass consists of an arpeggiation of I–III–V–I in the minor, but each of the scale-steps receives considerably more elaboration than in the previous piece of music.

In the first four measures the scale-step I is elaborated by its own complete harmonic unit of I–V–I. This is itself elaborated by a falling stepwise motion to the dominant in mm. 2–3. In a similar manner, the next scale step of III is decorated in mm. 6–11 by a V–I–V–I harmonic unit that takes us temporarily into E♭ major. At the end of the example, the bracketed C indicates that the piece arrives back in the tonic in (m. 13), but the music for this section is not included in the example.

Example 3.4 Haydn, Piano Sonata in C major, Hob. XVI, No. 10, Trio

Source: Based on the pattern suggested in Schenker 1977: Figure 26a

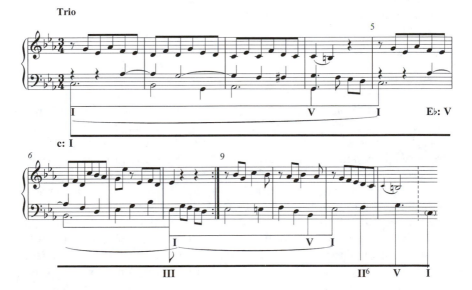

Tonicization

In traditional harmonic theory, mm. 6–11 would be described as a modulation to E♭. Schenker, however, is disdainful about the notion of modulation and replaces it with the concept of tonicization, in which a scale-step such as III becomes a temporary tonic. This emphasizes the relationship back to the main tonic and the notion of a large-scale linear-harmonic structure rather than simply a succession of chords in various keys. In this example then, III is tonicized by its dominant and by the contrapuntal setting of this scale-step.

The opening of the trio movement in Example 3.4 is just enough for us to get a glimpse, on this small scale, of how Schenker's bass prolongations correspond to traditional notions of form. The movement is in typical minor key binary form, in which an A section (mm. 1–8) modulating to the relative major is complemented by a B section (mm. 9 to the end) that moves to the dominant before returning to the tonic. Schenker's linear-harmonic approach reveals that the beginning of the B section in m. 9 continues a large-scale bass motion from the tonic that started in m. 1 and arrives on the dominant in m. 12. Notwithstanding the repeat mark then, Schenker would understand the first twelve measures as a continuous bass prolongation from I to V. Whereas we might be used to considering a repeat mark as an indication of an important formal division, for Schenker such a feature might merely be a foreground detail; the deeper structure is revealed by the contrapuntal elaboration of the bass.

Two-part contrapuntal structures

Having briefly explored bass structures, we can now explore how the *Bassbrechung* is brought together with an upper voice to create the very simple two-part counterpoint that appears at the deepest layer of a Schenkerian analysis. Schenker proposes a restricted set of simple patterns for the background structure, which he calls the *Ursatz* (usually translated as "fundamental structure") in which the upper voice is a descending linear progression, which he calls the *Urlinie* (translated as "fundamental line"). The simplest version of the *Ursatz* is shown in Example 3.5—a descent from the third degree of the scale to the root over the I–V–I of the *Bassbrechung*.

In proposing the *Ursatz*, Schenker is trying to demonstrate how tonal works grow out of this basic contrapuntal structure. The process of analyzing how a piece of music can be understood as an elaboration of the *Ursatz* sheds light on its large-scale shape and structure. From a Schenkerian

Example 3.5 The *Ursatz*

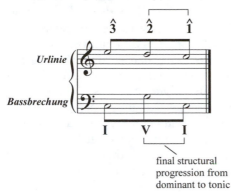

final structural
progression from
dominant to tonic

Notating the Ursatz

The *Urlinie* is highlighted in Schenkerian graphs by caretted numbers, which correspond to the degrees of the scale of the home tonic. The notes of the *Urlinie* are usually connected by stems and a heavy beam, as are the principal notes of the *Bassbrechung*. In addition, Roman numerals are used to label the principal harmonies; at this deep level they will always relate to the home tonic.

---

perspective it also aims to show how the music is drawn together by the *Ursatz*, how it can be understood as a unified whole. This goal is one shared by more traditional approaches such as sonata form or motivic analysis, which also attempt to show how a piece can be understood in terms of a single principle or structure. Although the traditional emphasis on unity has been criticized by some scholars as suppressing other (more) interesting aspects of music, curiosity about the way in which a work is pulled together by its internal logic is nevertheless an important part of the aesthetic of many of the composers with whom Schenker is concerned.[1]

Closure and the descending line

The *Ursatz* evolved over a number of years as Schenker developed his theory by analyzing a large number of tonal works. The rationale behind its final form is complex and involved, but it is worth briefly considering why Schenker settled on the descending line as the *Urlinie*. It is an important article of faith for Schenkerian theory that melodic lines ending on the first degree of the scale ($\hat{1}$) feel more closed and final than those that do not. As early as 1906, Schenker was writing that to come to a close on the third or the fifth of the chord offers an "inferior degree of satisfaction."[2] For Schenker, it is not until a work has closed on $\hat{1}$ that its tonal tensions are finally resolved. It is noteworthy that many hymns, nursery rhymes and national songs do in fact end on the first degree of the scale, and large swathes of the tonal canon do so also. Of the 370 harmonized chorales by Bach in Riemenschneider's collection, for example, only 3 percent do not end on a root position chord with $\hat{1}$ in the soprano voice.[3] It is interesting that these simple but highly influential melodies (mostly drawn from melodies in regular use by the Lutheran church in Bach's time) have such a high percentage of endings on $\hat{1}$, but even in Beethoven's highly sophisticated and individual set of thirty-two piano sonatas there are only eighteen individual movements that do not end on $\hat{1}$, and only five of those are final movements.[4]

Example 3.6 shows a few examples of closure onto $\hat{1}$ from the repertoire in which Schenker was most interested—common practice tonal music from Bach to Brahms. As with all but four of Bach's series of forty-eight fugues from *The Well-tempered Clavier*, the E♭ major from the first book ends by settling onto a tonic chord with $\hat{1}$ at the top (Example 3.6a).[5] As you would expect from Classical composers, both the Mozart and Beethoven examples make more of a dramatic point of their endings than Bach, but the flourish at the end of *The Magic Flute* overture and the rather more coy conclusion to Beethoven's Piano Sonata, Op. 49, No. 2 both involve a final $\hat{1}$. The extract from Brahms' First Symphony is the conclusion to eight pages that are largely concerned with hammering home the tonic—the final chord in such endings is almost always voiced with $\hat{1}$ at the top (Example 3.6d).

It is partly this feature of tonal closure that led Schenker to propose a large-scale linear progression ending on $\hat{1}$ as his basic model. Example 3.7 explores some simple embellishments of this archetypal closing gesture. In Example 3.7b, $\hat{2}$ is decorated by a descending third progression (D–B) that elaborates the dominant. Example 3.7c, on the other hand, embellishes the harmony by adding a first inversion chord II before the dominant, a common harmonic approach to a perfect cadence. This chord II can also be understood as an incomplete neighbor-note embellishment (the bass note F) of the root of the dominant (G). Example 3.7d combines these two embellishments, while Example 3.7e supports the dissonant passing note (C) with a cadential six-four onto the dominant.

The Baroque and Classical repertoires contain a huge number of similarly modest variants of this archetypal $\hat{2}$–$\hat{1}$ over a perfect cadence. However, Example 3.8, from the end of one of Chopin's piano preludes, is much more extravagant in the way that it extends the closing gesture found in Example 3.7b. The embellishment of $\hat{2}$ by a descending third progression is drawn

Example 3.6 Examples of endings on Î (last few measures of each)

(a) J. S. Bach, *The Well Tempered Clavier*, Book I, Fugue VII

(b) Mozart, *The Magic Flute*, Overture

(c) Beethoven, Piano Sonata, Op. 49, No. 2, Tempo di Menuetto

(d) Brahms, Symphony No. 1, Finale

out over five measures. In the first measure of the extract the initial $\hat{2}$ over the dominant is simply prolonged by a 4–3 suspension in one of the middle voices but the passing note E is subjected to a series of delaying elaborations.

Example 3.8 is based on the same archetype of $\hat{2}$ to $\hat{1}$ over a perfect cadence as the Bach Fugue ending in Example 3.6a. Although the dignified contrapuntal splendor of the fugue is very different to the drawn-out romantic

Example 3.7 Different embellishments of a $\hat{2}-\hat{1}$ ending

yearning of Chopin's prelude, their closing gesture is essentially the same. This idea of similarity and variety is central to Schenker's fascination with tonal music: in the words of the motto introduced in Chapter 1, "always the same but not in the same way." The Chopin is also a dramatic example of the idea that arrival on $\hat{1}/I$ is a moment of resolution. For Schenker, the

Example 3.8 Chopin, Prelude, Op. 28, No. 4, final measures

beginning of his descending *Urlinie* (the 3̂ in Example 3.5) introduces a tension that is sustained across the entire piece until its resolution by the arrival on 1̂.

A Schenkerian analysis of a passage does not therefore stand on its own but has to be understood in the context of similar passages from other pieces. The *Ursatz* is a common denominator, representing voice-leading patterns found in a wide range of music. In the process of relating a given passage to the structures proposed by Schenker, we discover what is distinctive about a particular piece of music. Schenkerian analysis is comparative, offering analytical insights that depend on parallels drawn across the tonal repertoire.

Two main purposes for the *Ursatz* with its descending *Urlinie* have emerged from this discussion: first, as a way of understanding pieces of music as a unified whole embodying a tension from its beginning to its end; second, as a tool for comparing how composers find different ways of elaborating on the same basic structures. Re-imagining music in these terms opens a fresh perspective on both the large-scale shape of tonal works and also their intricate details.

To return to practicalities, Example 3.9 provides a clear illustration of some basic features of *Ursatz* elaborations. The descending melodic step from the second degree of the scale (2̂) to the tonic (1̂) is always supported both contrapuntally and harmonically by the falling fifth to the tonic (V–I).

Example 3.9 A short phrase based on the *Ursatz*

In the very short example in Example 3.9, the $\hat{2}$–$\hat{1}$ of the *Urlinie* is the final perfect cadence of the phrase. Although this can also be the case in a longer extract, the descent of the *Urlinie* to $\hat{1}$ and the accompanying V–I does not necessarily have to be right at the end of the piece. One example might be coda sections, which can occur after the final descent onto $\hat{1}$, elaborating and emphasizing the arrival on the tonic.

In the case of an *Urlinie* descending from $\hat{3}$ (as in Example 3.9), this means that most of the music in a given piece is taken up with expanding the initial $\hat{3}$ in various ways and elaborating the gap between I and V. As shown in Example 3.9b the first elaboration in this phrase is a rising third up to the $\hat{3}$ that expands the initial tonic. $\hat{3}$ is then elaborated by an upper neighbor note that is supported in the bass by a neighbor note approach to the dominant, which creates a few beats of subdominant harmony. In a full-length example from a real piece of music, each of these simple elaborations could themselves be subject to further expansions, stretching the *Ursatz* out across a whole piece.

Variants of the *Urlinie*

The descent from $\hat{3}$ is only one of three basic forms of the *Urlinie*, as shown in Example 3.10. The *Bassbrechung* remains the same in each case, but the

Example 3.10 Descents from $\hat{3}$, $\hat{5}$ and $\hat{8}$

Unsupported stretch

One of the criteria for deciding which *Kopfton* is most appropriate is the extent to which the notes of the *Urlinie* are contrapuntally and harmonically supported by the bass. In the descent from $\hat{5}$ in its most basic form aligned over I–V–I, the $\hat{4}$ is not supported by the bass. The span between $\hat{5}$ and $\hat{3}$ is therefore sometimes referred to as the "unsupported stretch" (*Leerlauf*). For an analysis showing a descent from $\hat{5}$, contrapuntal support for this stretch is therefore important if it is to be convincing. This requirement means that, in practice, descents from $\hat{3}$ are the most common whereas properly supported descents from $\hat{8}$ are very rare indeed.

---

descent begins from a different head tone (or *Kopfton*). These diatonic structures all ultimately represent contrapuntal realizations of the tonic chords shown at the end of each descent, filling out the space between the notes from the tonic with passing notes. The (X) marked in the bass parts between the initial I and the final V indicate that this is where one would expect harmonic elaborations. Clearly the *Urlinie* that have $\hat{5}$ or $\hat{8}$ as their *Kopfton* theoretically present more opportunities for contrapuntal and thus harmonic elaboration between I and V.

Schenker proposes a number of standard ways in which these three variants are generally elaborated, but before exploring these, it is worth considering a brief example of the *Ursatz* in practice, in order to give a flavor of how it can work. Example 3.11b shows the first four measures of a Chopin mazurka. Although it may seem rather a brief extract to be relevant to the background structure, it is the crucial phrase of the main section because varied repeats of this material appear twice at the beginning, twice in the middle and twice at the end. As we shall see when we return to the mazurka later in this chapter, this descending fifth figure turns out to be the main descent of the *Urlinie* from $\hat{5}$ to $\hat{1}$.

Example 3.11 Chopin, Mazurka, Op. 17, No. 1

The first lesson to be learnt from this example is that the descending notes of the *Urlinie* are not usually distributed evenly. In this passage, $\hat{5}$ is decorated by two lower neighbor notes that span over a measure, after which $\hat{4}$ and $\hat{3}$ occupy only one quarter beat each; finally, both $\hat{2}$ and $\hat{1}$ are elaborated for three beats each. Although slightly longer, the elaborations of $\hat{5}$, $\hat{2}$ and $\hat{1}$ are still very simple, with only one chord per scale degree; it is quite common for the elaboration of $\hat{5}$, for example, to involve a lengthy and complex passage after which the music might make comparatively rapid progress through the remainder of the descent to $\hat{1}$.

Another issue worth considering is the fact that one needs to have Schenker's background model in mind in order to arrive at this interpretation—it is not the inevitable outcome of a purely mechanical analysis of the surface. If one were not looking for a descent in this passage, it would be logical (although not necessarily particularly musical) to consider m. 3 as an elaboration of E♭ and the final two measures as an elaboration of D. There are definite advantages to the analysis shown in Example 3.11a (it is hard to hear m. 3 as an elaboration of E♭), but it is having the *Ursatz* model in mind that nevertheless tips the balance in favor of a descending fifth progression. From the point of view of Schenker's ideas about closure on $\hat{1}$, it is interesting that in the final repetition of this phrase at the end of the piece, Chopin reinforces the sense of arrival on B♭ by replacing the final D with a B♭ up the octave.

The main prolongations of the *Ursatz*

The rest of this chapter outlines some of the most common prolongations of these basic *Ursatz* structures, along with some brief examples. Longer examples are explored in later chapters, while the practical questions of how to approach background analysis are tackled in Chapter 4. Schenker calls the elaborations of the *Ursatz* outlined below the first-level middleground (i.e. the initial layer of elaboration as we work from deep structure to surface). Informally, analysts quite often refer to the *Ursatz* and its immediate prolongations as the background.

Compound melody and background prolongations

Because leaps usually represent a motion between different voices (see the discussions on compound melody and unfolding in the previous chapter), a leap in the first-level middleground introduces a new voice as shown in the example below. The skip from E to C, for example, is understood as an unfolding down into an inner voice and is perhaps the simplest way in which a note of the *Urlinie* can be prolonged. The unfolding is of a two-note chord that is folded back up in the second part of the example.

Many of the first-level middleground features discussed below (particularly linear progressions) can be understood as elaborations of this sort of unfolding. An example of this is shown in the final part of Example 3.12, in which the same unfolding is elaborated by third progressions. As in the foreground, there are two alternative notations: diagonal beams and stems or simply diagonal lines, if no elaborations of the unfolding are shown.

Initial arpeggiations and initial ascents

The reason why Schenker chooses the descending *Urlinie* as his primary structure is that, while most pieces can be shown to culminate in some sort of descending line, what happens before this descent (if anything) varies widely. Schenkerian theory identifies two particularly common ways in

Example 3.12 Unfoldings

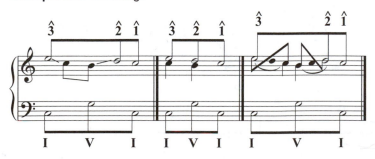

which the *Kopfton* (the initial note of the *Urlinie*) might be approached, shown in Example 3.13. Both of these first-level middleground elaborations create an overall arch-like shape by ascending to the *Kopfton* either by step or by leap. If, as Schenker suggests, arrival on $\hat{1}$ resolves the tension introduced by the *Kopfton* of $\hat{3}$ or $\hat{5}$, initial ascents and arpeggiations are a way of delaying the introduction of this tension in the first place.

Example 3.13a shows a stepwise approach to the *Kopfton*, which Schenkerians call an initial ascent (*Ansteig*). In this case the initial ascent is to $\hat{3}$, from which the *Urlinie* then descends as usual. An initial ascent might also rise from $\hat{1}$ or $\hat{3}$ to $\hat{5}$. Example 3.13b, on the other hand, is an example of an initial arpeggiation, which skips up through the pitches of the tonic chord to the *Kopfton*—in this case $\hat{5}$.

The opening of Schubert's "Wanderer's Nachtlied" shown in Example 3.14 is a good example of an initial ascent. The vocal line rises to $\hat{3}$ over the first three measures by means of a third progression. The initial ascent, marked with stems and a slur, is a first-level middleground feature as it directly prolongs the initial $\hat{3}$ of the *Urlinie* but it is elaborated in various ways in the foreground. The underlying pattern is of a series of reaching-over gestures marked by flagged stems in Example 3.14a, and these are further elaborated by rising third progressions that fill in the gaps. The basic harmonic support for the initial ascent is I–V–I, but this is embellished by means of a neighbor note to V at the beginning of m. 2 (chord II), which is reached by means of a descending skip through E as VI in the first measure.

The initial arpeggiation in Example 3.15 is elaborated more extensively. The arpeggiation is marked by a series of unfoldings as the melody in the right hand keeps returning to an inner voice A♭, but this does not detract from the clear sense of upwards progress to the A♭ in m. 14. Notice how the bass line switches from providing harmonic support to the right hand neighbor notes in m. 1 to being the main melody part at the end of m.3.

This passage includes a small-scale descent from the *Kopfton* of $\hat{5}$ to $\hat{1}$ in m. 16. This is a good example of what Schenker's model can tell us about the shape of a piece of music. From the perspective of the *Ursatz*, it takes

Example 3.13 Initial ascent and initial arpeggiation

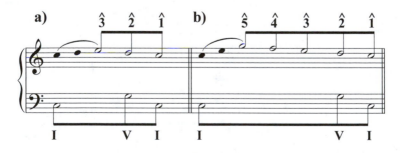

Example 3.14 Schubert, "Wanderer's Nachtlied," Op. 4, No. 3

Source: Based on Schenker 1977: Figure 37a

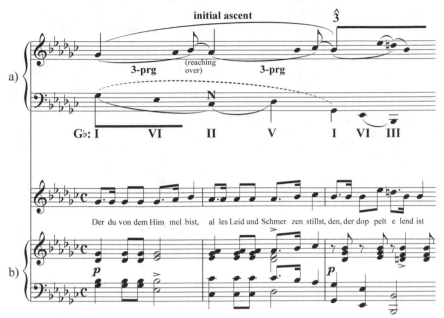

a whole fourteen measures to introduce the tension of $\hat{5}$ (more if the repeat is included), which is then resolved by descending to $\hat{1}$ in just three. The structural high point of the passage is therefore nearly at the end of the passage in m. 14, which is confirmed both by being the highest pitch so far and by being marked with the loudest dynamic. The tensional arch of Schenker's *Ursatz* is by no means always so clearly foregrounded; in this case, the analysis reveals that all the various structural and surface parameters are working together to produce this high point of tension.

Finally, it is worth noting the structure of the bass line in Example 3.15. It is an elaboration of the *Bassbrechung* model outlined in Example 3.2b: it moves from I at the beginning to I6 in m. 14 from which it moves by step up to the final dominant in the following measure.

Motion from and to an inner voice

Schenker suggests that all linear progressions that directly prolong the *Urlinie* in the first-level middleground must either *descend from* or *ascend to* one of its notes. As discussed above, linear progressions represent a motion between two voices, so the initial descending fifth progression in Example 3.16a moves from the G of the *Urlinie* to C in a lower voice (shown in brackets). Example 3.16b demonstrates why Schenker proscribes ascending

Example 3.15 Beethoven, Piano Sonata in F minor, Op. 57, Andante con moto

Source: Extrapolated from Schenker 1977: Figure 40/8

Just as the first note of a piece does not necessarily have to be the *Kopfton* of $\hat{3}$ or $\hat{5}$, so the final two notes do not have to be $\hat{2}$–$\hat{1}$. The last five measures of the Haydn sonata movement in the following example consist of a series of closing gestures that follow a clear descent to $\hat{1}$ in the third and fourth measures of the extract. Even without the *Ursatz*, it is clear that these gestures occur after the music has already come to some sort of close.

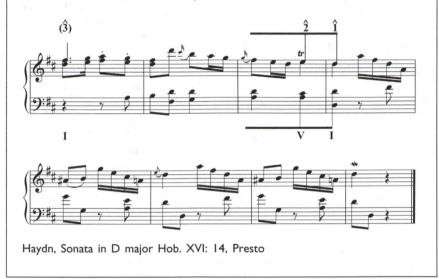

Haydn, Sonata in D major Hob. XVI: 14, Presto

Example 3.16 Motion from and to an inner voice

linear progressions from, or descending progressions to, a note of the *Urlinie* in the first-level middleground; in both cases this would introduce a new voice above the *Urlinie*. Although this might be common enough on the surface of the music (see reaching over on p. 44), Schenker is keen to not to spoil the clarity of the first-level middleground through the addition of new upper voices. Schenker calls the second progression in Example 3.16a "motion from the inner voice"—the initial ascent described above is simply a motion from the inner voice that arrives on the first note of the *Urlinie*.

Interruptions and neighbor notes

A common elaboration of an *Urlinie* from $\hat{3}$ is the upper neighbor note shown in Example 3.17a. In a shorter piece, the upper neighbor might generate only a fleeting elaboration of IV, but in a longer work this type of elaboration might give rise to a substantial passage of music. A three-part structure, for example, might involve a section in the tonic (the $\hat{3}$), followed by a trio or similar contrasting section in the subdominant (represented by the neighbor note) followed by a return of the opening material ($\hat{3}$) and the completion of the descent to $\hat{1}$.

Example 3.17b initially looks like a similar case with the F creating a lower neighbor note to $\hat{3}$. Schenker represents this type of elaboration with a different notation, however, because it plays such a crucial role in the structure of tonal music. It is very common for a piece to arrive on the dominant at a key structural point, such as the end of the A section of a binary or ternary form or the end of a sonata form exposition; the arrival on the first $\hat{2}$/V in Example 3.17b is often the point in the *Ursatz* elaboration at which such a structural dominant is reached. Schenker describes this articulation of the *Urlinie* as an *interruption*, because it interrupts the descending line by moving back up to the *Kopfton* (in this case $\hat{3}$) before resuming its descent. In a shorter work this may involve merely arrival on a half cadence, but in a more substantial piece it will probably involve a modulation to (or in Schenkerian terms a tonicization of) the dominant.

Example 3.17 Neighbor note and interruption

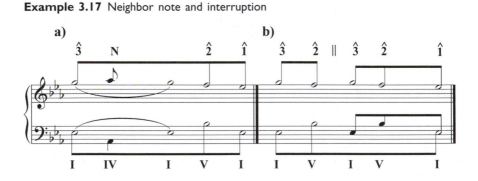

Schenker is keen to reflect in his notation the fact that the interruption is the division of a single unified structure. He stresses that the 3̂ after the interruption is a return rather than a "first attempt" at a complete descent; if the second I–V was not shown as subordinate (i.e. if it connected to the main beam), the return of 3̂ might look like a full close from V–I, an interpretation that Schenker forcefully rejects, partly because this would undermine his point that the interrupted *Urlinie* is still ultimately a single motion from beginning to end.

Interruptions of descents from 5̂ or 8̂ are also possible, in which case the interruption again involves arrival on 2̂ followed by a complete descent from the original *Kopfton*. Interruptions are shown by means of a double slash after the 2̂ and (usually) a breaking of the main beam that connects the notes of the *Urlinie*.

Schenker insists that only upper neighbor notes are possible in the first-level middleground, because a lower neighbor note to 3̂ would be an interruption while a lower neighbor note to 2̂ would complete the descent onto 1̂. At the deep level of immediate prolongations of the *Urlinie*, Schenker attempts to avoid the possibility of structural ambiguity.

Example 3.18 shows how the first phrase of the famous "Ode to Joy" theme from Beethoven's Ninth is based on an interruption structure—almost all of the large-scale elaborations outlined in this section can also be found close to the surface of the music in this way. The half cadence at

Example 3.18 Beethoven, Symphony No. 9, "Ode to Joy" theme from finale

Source: Based on Schenker 1977: Figure 109e3

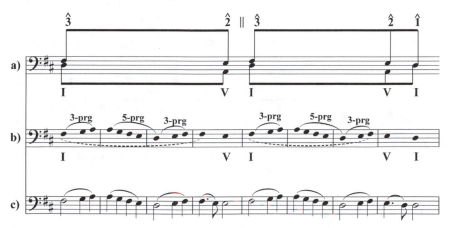

the end of m. 4 marks the point of interruption, after which the music restarts on $\hat{3}$ before continuing to a full cadence. This shows in miniature the close relationship between *Ursatz* elaborations and form: the idea of two closely related halves of a phrase with different degrees of tonal closure is clearly reflected in the representation of the structure in Example 3.18a.

Example 3.19 shows another interruption structure, this time decorated by an initial ascent to $\hat{3}$. The second part of the phrase includes a reaching over, as the melody leaps up to A at the end of the fourth measure in order to drop down by step onto the return of $\hat{3}$. This reaching over back onto $\hat{3}$ is a common feature and also demonstrates in miniature how music that immediately follows an interruption often functions from a Schenkerian point of view. The end of m. 3 and the beginning of m. 4 serve to heighten the tension of the dominant before the return of the $\hat{3}$ over the tonic on the third quarter of the fourth measure; in a sonata-form piece, the point of interruption would be at the end of the exposition, after which the entire development section would serve the same function as these few beats—to prolong the tension of V before the eventual return of the tonic.

Example 3.19 Mozart, Variations for Piano in D, KV 25

Example 3.19b has a number of slurs under the Roman numerals. These slurs show larger-scale harmonic units such as I–V–I, V–I and I–V. The rising third progression of the initial ascent up to the first quarter of m. 3, for example, prolongs the tonic so the harmonic unit of I–V–I is grouped together with a slur. Harmonic units that move from I–V are marked with a special type of slur that curls up and over the V, as seen at the end of the third measure. The notation of Schenkerian analysis is outlined systematically in the following chapter.

Example 3.20a shows another model for a neighbor-note elaboration of the Ursatz, this time involving an Urlinie descent from $\hat{5}$. The piece in question is the Chopin mazurka from which we saw an extract in Example 3.11 and the analysis is based on a background graph from Schenker's book *Free Composition* (Schenker 1977). Example 3.11 suggested that a descending-fifth passage that dominated the repeated A section could be understood as the main structural feature; the entire section is therefore represented by a single fifth progression in Example 3.20a. In between the two repeats of the A section is a much shorter B section, which again is quite repetitive. The main phrase of the B section, which elaborates a descending third progression over a tonic pedal, is shown in Example 3.20b. Apart from the various accented dissonances and chromatic embellishments, the main complication is that the first note of the third progression (the G) appears in a lower octave than the remaining two notes; shifts of register of this sort are discussed below.

The point is not to explore the intricate details of this piece but to get a sense of how a movement in several sections might be understood in terms of *Ursatz*. In this regard, the main feature to notice is that while the first A section is shown simply as a single descending fifth progression, when this section is repeated at the end of the mazurka the same progression is notated as an *Urlinie* descent. Although the music is not any different, this is its last appearance, so it is shown as the final descent to $\hat{1}$, the structural close of the piece. In one sense Schenker is merely representing graphically the fact that the piece is over when the phrase is repeated for the last time, which is obvious enough; at the same time this notation emphasizes his conceptualization of Chopin's mazurka (and all tonal works) as the elaboration of a single descent of the *Urlinie*. The B section of this ternary form is shown to be a decoration of this structure rather than something separate inserted in between two repetitions of the A section. The unity of the piece is emphasized over its division into several sections.

Example 3.20 Chopin, Mazurka, Op. 17, No. 1: (a) Analysis after Schenker;
(b) Mm. 57–60

Source: (a) based on Schenker 1977: Figure 76/5

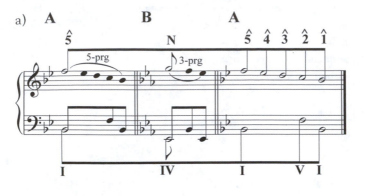

Obligatory register

One interesting feature of the *Ursatz* is Schenker's insistence that the *Urlinie* descent will always end in the same octave that it begins, a principle he calls the "obligatory register" (*Obligate Lage*). The importance of register as a form of elaboration in the foreground is easy to see in Example 3.21,

Example 3.21 Mozart, Piano Sonata in C minor, KV 457, Allegro assai

which shows a short passage from one of Mozart's piano sonatas. Over a repeating accompanying figure, the C in the right hand is elaborated by the simple device of repeating the neighbor-note motif from m. 278—an octave higher at m. 280 and then an octave lower two measures later. One often sees this device on a slightly larger scale when composers repeat whole phrases in different registers. Such local changes of octave might well be employed in order to exploit, for example, the differing colors available on the piano or the brilliant upper range of the violin or flute.

The idea of foreground changes of register can easily be translated into the middleground and background, with a note of the *Urlinie* repeated or transferred into a different octave, as shown in the next section of this chapter. Schenker goes further than this, however, in suggesting that moving away from a given register introduces a tension that ultimately needs to be resolved by returning to that register. He writes that a piece of music "retains an urge to return to" the obligatory register and consequently that the movement from and return to this register "creates content, displays the instrument and lends coherence to the whole."[6] A change from one register to another therefore generates musical interest by moving away from the hypothetical single register of the background. At the same time, the unity of the surface layers is ensured by their derivation from simple prolongations of the *Ursatz*, which is ultimately a contrapuntal realization of a tonic chord. As so often with Schenkerian thought, this all makes much better sense if you think of the musical process of elaboration from background to foreground rather than the analytical journey in the opposite direction.

From a practical point of view, the notion of obligatory register affirms that ultimately a piece of music will be comprehensible from the point of view of a simple *Urlinie* descent within a single octave. This might seem problematic, raising the question of what happens if a piece does not close in the original register. Is Schenker suggesting that pieces in violation of the obligatory register are compositional mistakes? In practice, this theoretical problem is not as thorny as one might expect. In the first instance, as in Example 3.22b, composers quite often reinforce closure in a number of registers, which makes it relatively easy to satisfy the principle of obligatory register. In addition, if a piece does seem to violate this principle, it might well tell us something interesting about the way the music works.

Example 3.22 Haydn, Piano Sonata in D major, Hob. XVI, No. 19, Moderato:
(a) Beginning; (b) End

The first movement of Haydn's D major piano sonata provides a typical example of the first case, as shown in Example 3.22. The work starts with a clear melodic statement in a single register and a Schenkerian analyst would therefore expect the *Urlinie* (presumably descending from F♯ as $\hat{3}$ in D major) to close in this octave.

A brief look at the final measures of the movement as shown in Example 3.22b, reveals that it ends with the right hand plunging down to a low D beneath the left hand accompaniment. This is clearly not an arrival on D as $\hat{1}$ in the obligatory register; neither is the preceding cadential figure, which is an octave too high. The previous measures, however, land twice on the "correct" D in clear cadential figures. From a Schenkerian point of view, the final two gestures are reinforcements of this D rather than representing a structural arrival on $\hat{1}$. As is often the case in such situations, this accords quite well with an intuitive reading of the music in any case, as the end of the penultimate measure is merely a repeat of what we have already heard an octave higher. The final Ds are also a reinforcing gesture, appearing well after the final arrival on the tonic and below the main accompanying figure. Schenker's principle of obligatory register therefore sharpens our understanding of the structure of the music at the end of the movement rather than being the apparently rather abstract and unintuitive idea that it might initially seem to be.

Register transfer and coupling

As with all Schenkerian concepts, extending changes of register into the deep structure of a piece assumes that a musical surface can and should be understood as the elaboration of a deeper layer. As shown in Example 3.23, Schenker suggests two distinct ways in which changes of register can be interpreted as elaborations of an *Ursatz* form. In Example 3.23a, three notes from the first part of an interrupted descent from $\hat{5}$ are transferred up the octave. Schenker calls this register transfer because the structural notes are simply shifted to a different octave—the principle of obligatory register is not ultimately violated because the final descent occurs in the same register as the beginning.[7]

Example 3.23b, on the other hand, shows a special type of register transfer that Schenker calls coupling. Here a note from the *Urlinie* is repeated (or coupled) at a lower register. Whereas register transfers tend to be a relatively local phenomena, a coupling (*Koppelung*) can be a major structural feature of a piece as the music first exploits one register and then the other.

The beginning of the Haydn minuet shown in Example 3.24 shows several types of register transfer in a single *Urlinie* descent from $\hat{5}$. The piece starts with a series of arpeggiations that introduce the initial $\hat{5}$ (D) across three different octaves. The middle of these three is the register in which the descent finally comes to a close on $\hat{1}$ at the end of the passage, so it is this D that is marked with a stem and caretted number. The other two Ds can be considered as local register transfers that add a bit of color. The transfer of $\hat{4}$ down an octave in m. 4, however, is more significant, because the *Urlinie* remains in this register for the following $\hat{3}$, which is the only instance of this pitch (B) in any register at this point. The lower of the two $\hat{4}$s is not connected to the main beam and bracketed because it is still only a

---

Note that the coupling in Example 3.23b is notated in the same manner as an unfolding. This draws attention to the fact that the second E and the first D are notionally in a lower voice—the beam and reversed stems reflect this switch from upper to lower voice and back again. In the middleground, particularly when the analysis is showing lots of foreground detail, couplings are usually shown using dotted slurs as in Example 3.25.

Example 3.23 Register transfer and coupling

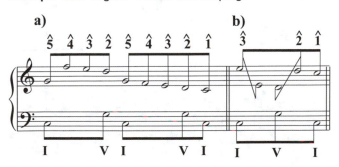

decoration of the same pitch in the upper register, but the $\hat{3}$ is connected to the beam because it is the sole representative of this part of the descent. The *Urlinie* stays in this lower register for its arrival on $\hat{2}$ in the following measure, but this is then transferred up to the main register after which the descent continues to its conclusion. The point at which a register transfer becomes a coupling is subjective and based on whether the change of octave connects two registers that are significant in the piece as a whole or not. Here the transfer of $\hat{3}$ does drag instances of $\hat{2}$ and $\hat{4}$ down the octave with it, but the development of this lower register is not extensive enough for this to be considered a coupling.

Dotted slurs are important for notating connections between the same pitch within and between registers. The D naturals at the beginning and end of the first two measures are connected with a dotted slur as are the $\hat{4}$s in different registers in the third and fourth measures. If two notes an octave apart are connected in the same elaboration as in the arpeggiation from D to D at the beginning, there is no need for a dotted slur because they are already connected by a solid one. Similarly, if two consecutive notes are at the same pitch in two different octaves, they should be joined with an ordinary slur; dotted slurs only show where notes are not directly connected but nevertheless related by being the same pitch. The implication of such a slur is that the elaboration of the first note is continued by the second; the triplet A at the end of the fourth measure, for example, cannot be connected with the A two measures later.

Example 3.24 Haydn, *Twelve Minuets*, Hob. IX, No. 11, Minuet No. 3

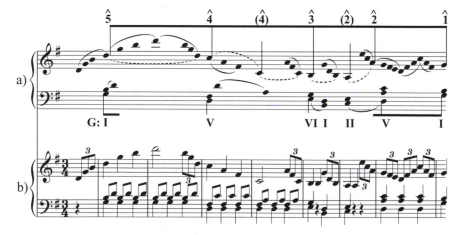

Example 3.25 shows the elaboration of $\hat{4}$ at the beginning of an early Mozart piano piece. The $\hat{5}$ at the beginning is connected up into a higher register and then transferred back down again at the end of the passage. This register transfer has the potential to develop into a coupling so long as these two registers continue to be exploited in the remainder of the work. This is a very short piece, and this is, in fact, the last that we hear of the upper octave, which means that this is simply a register transfer after all. The difference between the two cannot be determined in such short extracts but only by looking at the context of the whole piece. The use of register as a compositional device is explored more fully in Chapter 8.

Mixture

Example 3.26 shows an elaboration of the *Ursatz* that Schenker calls mixture (*Mischung*), because it mixes minor with major. The graph is an analysis of a minuet and trio by Haydn, the structural outlines of which are shown in Example 3.27. The minuet is a complete descent from $\hat{3}$ in E major (Example 3.27a) and is followed by a trio (Example 3.27b) in the parallel minor, which also describes a descent from $\hat{3}$. As shown in Example 3.26, most of the piece is therefore understood as an elaboration of $\hat{3}$. As the minuet is repeated, the first and last sections are exactly the same piece of music; as in previous examples, however, the third progression it entails is first interpreted as a middleground closure at the beginning and then as the *Urlinie* descent at the end. Such small-scale replications of *Ursatz*-like

Example 3.25 Mozart, *The London Sketchbook*, KV 15, No. 12

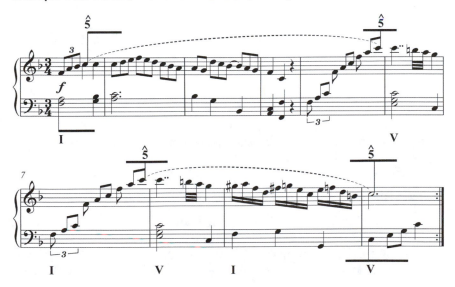

Example 3.26 Mixture and ternary form

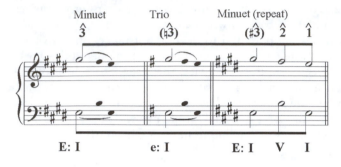

Example 3.27 Haydn, *Twelve Minuets*, Hob. IX, No. 11, Minuet No. 4

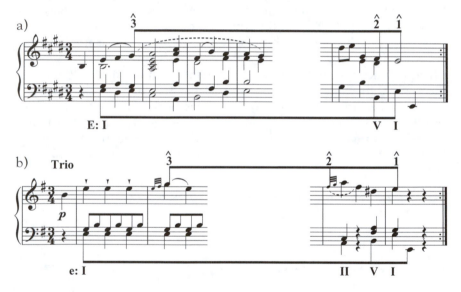

structures in the middleground of pieces of tonal music are common; they differ from a true *Ursatz* only in that they do not span a whole piece.

Some further prolongations of the *Bassbrechung*

The middleground prolongations detailed so far have mostly focused on embellishment of the *Urlinie*. We have already seen how the most basic *Bassbrechung* elaborations involve filling in the gap between the initial tonic and the final dominant, but there are many possible variants of this scheme.

Example 3.28 shows some simple elaborations of a modified *Bassbrechung* pattern in which the bass descends to the dominant rather than ascends; the emphasis is on how the gap between I and V is elaborated melodically and thus generates new harmonies. Example 3.28b fills in the falling fourth with passing notes, and Example 3.28c consists of an arpeggiation down from I to IV before proceeding to the dominant. Example 3.28d is a bit more complicated, with the gap between I and V in G minor being composed out by two linear-harmonic units. The first elaborates the initial tonic by means of an arpeggiation, while the second moves stepwise to the dominant, creating a rising third progression. These are themselves expanded with further elaborations—two neighbor notes (F♯ and E) and a chromatic passing note (B).

The Bach chorale extract in Example 3.29 is a composing-out of Example 3.28c. The bass line outlines the same arpeggiation from I down to IV, but the gaps are filled in with passing notes. Chord IV is then briefly tonicized by its dominant to form a complete harmonic unit as indicated by the slur beneath the Roman numerals. In the final measure this subdominant chord becomes the approach chord to a perfect cadence. We have already encountered Schenker's motto "always the same but not in the same way," and these archetypal bass structures are a very good example of this in practice. Schenker wants to show how musical phrases—and ultimately pieces—are based on a small number of simple patterns, but he is fascinated by the infinitely various ways in which they can be elaborated. In Example 3.29 the distinguishing feature of the phrase is the proportionately quite long prolongation of chord IV.

A final type of *Bassbrechung* prolongation worth mentioning is where the entire bass structure is repeated under a single *Urlinie*. In Example 3.30 the I–V–I is repeated under an *Urlinie* descent from $\hat{5}$. The gap between I and V is elaborated by the dominant being approached through the step of a second—the first time this results in chord IV and the second time chord II. The repeated *Bassbrechung* is sometimes notated with connecting diagonal lines as shown in the example.

Example 3.28 Examples of I–V–I structures descending

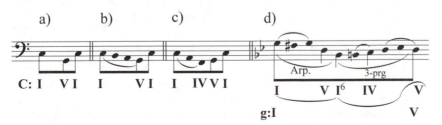

Example 3.29 J. S. Bach, Chorale "Der Tag, der is so freudenrich" (Riemenschneider No. 158)

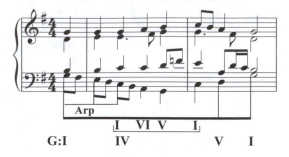

Example 3.30 Double arpeggiation in bass

Substitution and cover tones

It is impossible to do justice to the all of the intricate complexities of Schenker's theory in this overview, but I have at least outlined the major ideas that underpin Schenkerian analysis. I am going to conclude by looking at extracts from two Brahms waltzes. As well as containing some of the features outlined above, they also raise some interesting issues relating to the analytical use of the *Ursatz*, in particular those cases in which the notes of the *Urlinie* do not actually appear in the music.

Schenker analyzes the second of Brahms's Op. 39 waltzes as a descent from $\hat{3}$ in E major with an interruption. The first half of the piece (shown in Example 3.31) displays one of the transformations of the *Ursatz* discussed above: the $\hat{2}$ at the end of the phrase is subject to a register transfer up the octave. Whereas the initial $\hat{3}$ appears in a straightforward manner over the tonic, by the time we arrive on the final dominant chord of this section, the top line has skipped down into an inner voice. This sort of displacement is quite a common device used by Schenkerian analysts; although the piece

Example 3.31 Brahms, Waltz, Op. 39, No. 2, mm. 1–8

Source: Based on Schenker 1977: Figure 46/1

does not actually progress to $\hat{2}$ over the dominant, it can easily be understood as a variant of this basic structure. As already discussed, the validity of this sort of interpretation relies on sharing Schenker's interest in showing how the tonal repertoire can be understood as variations on the same basic patterns.

Example 3.32 shows how, after a central section that is not included here, the music from the beginning returns. This time, however, it is modified so that it ends in the tonic rather than the dominant and, unsurprisingly, Schenker interprets this as the completion of the interrupted *Urlinie* descent. However, there are several ways in which the surface of the music does not completely match up with the analysis, including the G♯ in the second measure of the extract, which appears an octave higher in the analysis than it does in the music. The most notable discrepancy, however, and one of the reasons why Schenker includes this analysis in *Free Composition*, is the complete absence of an F♯ in the penultimate measure of the music. Although the waltz ends on a clear $\hat{1}$ in the last measure, the dominant that precedes

Example 3.32 Brahms, Waltz, Op. 39, No. 2, mm. 16–24

Source: Based on Schenker 1977: Ex. 46/1

it as part of the cadence does not have a $\hat{2}$ from which to descend to this final melody note. Schenker writes that "the counterpointing bass arpeggiation [i.e. the dominant at the end of m. 23] clearly indicates the actual tone of the fundamental line, even though it is hidden" (Schenker 1977: 51). Although there is no descent through $\hat{2}$ to $\hat{1}$ at the end of this piece, Schenker uses the concept of substitution to suggest that it is nevertheless conceptually present.

If you accept the importance of Schenker's model of a descending progression from $\hat{3}$ through $\hat{2}$ to $\hat{1}$, then this substitution is not much more problematic than the many other foreground elaborations of this archetype we have seen. A more pragmatic argument along similar lines is that our tendency (or ability) to "hear" underlying simple stepwise connections means that we conceptually fill in the gap between the clearly present $\hat{3}$ and $\hat{1}$ in order to hear the phrase as a single linear progression from beginning to end. Although these two arguments rely on a prior acceptance of Schenker's models, they are logical in their own terms, the substituted $\hat{2}$ being understood as what might be described as an elaboration by omission.

Example 3.33 shows the beginning and end of a Brahms waltz. At the opening, the main melodic interest is clearly not at the top of the texture— the uppermost part simply repeats the B naturals, as does the tenor voice. If we were analyzing the opening of this piece in terms of the *Ursatz*, we would therefore probably concentrate on the alto, in which the principal melody is presented. In Schenkerian parlance the B is called a cover tone (*Deckton*), because it covers the main voice.

The end of the waltz is perhaps not so clear-cut; if you heard this passage on its own, the alto would not so obviously be the principal voice. Nevertheless there are two reasons to interpret it in this way: first, a clear precedent is set at the opening; and second, in order to understand the piece in terms of Schenker's model of tonal closure (i.e. stepwise from $\hat{2}$ to $\hat{1}$). The suggestion is not that the top line should be ignored or is unimportant, merely that it should be understood in its context as an embellishing voice that disguises the more "usual" stepwise closure.

Although substitutions and cover tones are perhaps conceptually difficult by comparison with the straightforward embellishments with which we started in Chapter 2, they are underpinned by the same basic idea of trying to understand music as the elaboration of simple models. The next chapters outline a step-by-step method for starting an analysis. Success in this discipline comes from careful and methodical work at the preparatory stage combined with having the imagination and flexibility to see how a piece might be understood from a Schenkerian point of view.

Example 3.33 Brahms, Waltz, Op. 39, No. 5

Part II

Getting started on an analysis

Chapter 4

A four-stage method

An introduction to the analytical process

Schenkerian analysis is a subtle art rather than a systematic science, but it is still possible to approach it in a methodical way. This chapter suggests thinking about your work in four interconnected stages; it should help you to get started, particularly if you are struggling to get to grips with the process of analysis.

The two main analytical procedures at the heart of Schenkerian analysis are essentially quite straightforward: identifying harmonic units (from chords to large-scale progressions) and exploring how these harmonic units are realized contrapuntally by linear units that are made up of various combinations of arpeggiations, neighbor notes and linear progressions. These procedures are complicated, first, by the multiple layers on which analysis operates and, second, by Schenker's insistence that the deepest layers of music consist of a small number of basic structures in the form of the *Ursatz*.

Before examining the process of identifying harmonic and contrapuntal structures in detail, it is worth looking at a very brief and simple example. The extract from a Haydn piano sonata shown in Example 4.1 is obviously too short to require sophisticated analytical work, but it nevertheless shows quite clearly the basic principles involved. Example 4.1 also demonstrates the four broad stages of analytical work proposed in this chapter.

You should be clear that the four stages outlined here are only a proposed method for getting started—they do not appear in this form anywhere in Schenker's publications. You should not, therefore, refer to them when writing about Schenkerian theory and analysis, but rather to foreground, middleground and background.

Example 4.1 Haydn, Piano Sonata in G major, Hob. XVI, No. 39, first movement

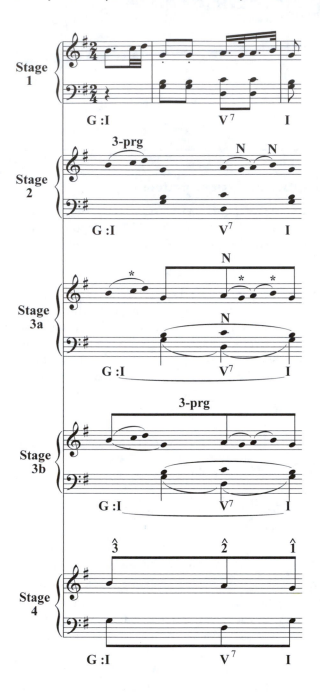

Stage 1: Foreground harmonic analysis

The notation of Schenkerian analysis strongly privileges the linear aspect of tonal music, but an understanding of the harmonic structure of a passage is vital to any meaningful analytical work. As shown in Example 4.1 a harmonic analysis is best done on a copy of the music itself, writing the relevant Roman numerals and figured bass below the staff. A Schenkerian analysis requires a good understanding of harmonic structure, so it is worth making a serious effort to complete this stage of the process thoroughly. This does not mean, however, that you need to find a harmonic label for every single vertical arrangement of notes.

Stage 2: Preparation of score and identification of foreground elaborations

The second stage of analysis is essentially preparatory: ensuring that you begin with some clarity about the surface of the music avoids building in mistakes as the analysis proceeds.

This first part of stage two is to prepare a stripped-down version of the score on which to notate the analysis:

1   Strip out the rhythmic notation and bar lines, leaving a series of filled unstemmed note heads—this leaves plenty of room for analytical notation.
2   Remove consecutively repeated notes, for example, the repeated G chord on the second quaver of the first full measure. Again, the point is to avoid having a cluttered analysis that is hard to interpret

The second part of stage two is to identify elaborations on the surface of the music. At this stage you are simply looking for groups of consecutive notes that can be understood to elaborate individual chords. The first three notes, for example, embellish the opening tonic harmony, while a series of neighbor notes decorates the A (from chord V) in the second half of the first full measure. It is vital that these elaborations make sense in terms of the harmony you are suggesting that they embellish.

The main point of this stage is to try and eliminate notes that are unlikely to form a part of deeper layers of your analysis. The thirty-second note C at the beginning, for example, is dissonant with the tonic and clearly a passing note between B and D. Slurring it into a foreground third progression helps to make clear in the next stages of your analysis what notes are unlikely to be significant in the middleground or background of the music. You might occasionally need to revise your surface analysis of the music, but it is better to have to change your mind than not to have an understanding of the surface of the music in the first place.

Stage 3: Middleground layer analysis

It is in stage three that you start the analysis properly; you have to be flexible and creative as you shuttle back and forth between the foreground and middleground layers. In addition, you need to look forward to the fourth and final stage of the analysis, in which you finally decide on the basic *Ursatz* form.

In essence, you are looking for larger-scale linear patterns that make sense of similarly large-scale harmonic units. The only available larger-scale harmonic unit in this short extract is the I–V–I arpeggiation, which is shown by a slur beneath the Roman numerals from I to I. As the principal harmony of this unit is the tonic, any linear elaborations should make sense as an elaboration of this chord. The first attempt at stage three (Stage 3a) finds two such elaborations: a neighbor note in the top voice and a similar figure in the middle voice. Unlike the foreground elaborations of stage two, it is usual for each part of a contrapuntal figure to have some harmonic support; here, both neighbor notes are supported by the dominant harmony in the second half of the measure. Part of the point of stage two is that you have already eliminated some notes from consideration, in this case the dissonant notes marked by asterisks on the example.

Although the neighbor note in the first attempt at stage three makes sense, it is not necessarily the best solution. The second attempt (Stage 3b) is better for two reasons: first, it encompasses the whole passage; and second, (looking ahead to stage four) it conforms to the descending third of one of Schenker's suggested *Ursatz* models. The second attempt at stage three extends further back than the G at the beginning of the first full measure, and finds a way to make a longer span in the shape of a descending third progression; the first four notes are now understood as an elaboration of the initial B—first by means of a foreground ascending third progression to G (already identified in stage two) and then by a skip into a lower voice G.

The slurs that connect the Roman numerals into harmonic units help you to ensure that your linear analysis makes tonal sense. You will find that slurs (and sometimes lines) are used sporadically by Schenker to show how harmonies are connected. In the rest of the professional literature the incidence of such slurs is also quite patchy—the advantage of harmonic clarity is arguably outweighed by an inevitable clutter. These harmonic slurs to some extent duplicate information that can easily be inferred from the rest of the analysis; while I strongly recommend their use as part of the process, it is a matter of taste how many you leave in the final version of your analysis.

Stage 4: Background analysis

Stage four involves making a final decision on the overarching *Ursatz* structure that your analysis is going to propose, something not particularly relevant in such a short example. The last two stages overlap considerably and you will find yourself moving between them several times, trying to reconcile different *Ursatz* possibilities with various ways of interpreting the middleground layers. In this very short extract, the *Ursatz* form is fairly obvious, but the principle is nevertheless the same as in an analysis of a whole piece. Although a piece of music will never only be two measures long, mini-*Ursatz* patterns in the middleground are actually quite common. In the rest of this chapter, the four stages are explained in detail.

Stages one and two

Stage one summary (foreground harmonic analysis)

- Label harmonies using Roman numerals and, where necessary, figured bass (it is often helpful to show first inversions and six-four chords using figured bass).
- Where a piece modulates, identify chords according to the local key. At later stages of the analysis, modulations will be re-interpreted as tonicizations—an E minor passage in the context of C major, for example, would be shown as a tonicization of III.

Stage two summary (preparation of score and identification of foreground elaborations)

Preparation of score:

- Represent each note with a stemless quarter note head.
- Remove bar lines.
- Remove consecutively repeated notes or phrases as appropriate.

Foreground elaborations:

- Identify any direct elaborations of foreground harmonies with slurs and appropriate labels:
  - arpeggiation (Arp.)
  - linear progressions (3-prg, 4-prg, etc.)
  - neighbor notes (N)
- Re-write more elaborate compound melodies, particular bass figurations, as chords (see Example 4.4).
- Identify any other foreground features that do not fall into the above categories, for example chromatic passing notes or suspensions.

Example 4.2, which is again very short, shows the first two stages in action and also looks forward to the third stage of analysis. Stage one is not too challenging in that the harmony stays on the tonic of D major. Notice that it is not necessary to label every single passing harmony—the C♯ and E in the first measure, for example, imply chord V. Including such details would make the task very tedious and, in any case, such brief harmonic allusions are usually better understood from a linear perspective (the C♯ is, for example, a neighbor note).

The first part of stage two is again reasonably straightforward in this example—the only notes omitted are the final three Ds in the bass part. They are deleted because they are simply a consecutive repeat of the leaping octave figure; including the repeat of this figure does not provide any extra information.

The second part of stage two involves finding linear units that elaborate the harmonies. Although a tonic pedal D underpins the whole passage, it makes sense to interpret the E and C♯ in the second half of the first full bar as an implied dominant harmony. The top part begins with a complete

Example 4.2 Clementi, Sonatina for Piano, Op. 38, No. 1

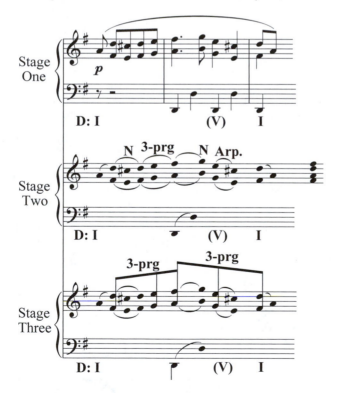

neighbor-note figure that then goes straight into a rising third progression. The G in the following measure is interpreted as an incomplete upper neighbor note to the F♯ and the C♯ at the end of the measure as an incomplete lower neighbor to the following D.

The A naturals at the beginning and end of the extract represent skips between the main voice and a notional lower one—a fleeting example of compound melody. The chord at the end of the upper stage two staff shows the four notional voices that the two actual upper parts involve. The lower part elaborates around the two lower voices and the upper part around the top two—the only exceptions are these A naturals, which represent brief excursions by the uppermost part into a lower voice. This sort of simple foreground skip between voices can be marked in stage two simply with a slur. The lower of the two parts does not require much comment as it shadows the upper part for the whole passage in parallel sixths.

The final staffs of Example 4.2 look briefly ahead to stage three, in which larger-scale elaborations are marked with stems and beams. Notice how the beginning has been re-interpreted to make it simpler: the initial neighbor note is now shown as a decoration of the initial D of the third progression, rather than as a completely separate elaboration. This reading suggests that the first part of the phrase is best understood as a single rising progression rather than as a series of consecutive elaborations of D major. The second half of the passage is tied together in a similar way, this time by a descending third progression. The ascending and falling third progressions both correspond to the D major tonic chord in that their first and last notes are both notes from that harmony. In this short example, the passing E naturals are not supported other than by the merest hint of the dominant in the lower voice in the right hand. True middleground linear progressions and

---

Overlapping

The last note of one progression in the foreground may or may not be shared with the first of the next as shown in the first two examples below. What is not possible is an actual overlap between elaborations. There are two reasons why the final example below is impossible: first, the rising fourth from D to G cannot be a prolongation of a D harmony; second, and more importantly, the G cannot be the consonant end note of a linear progression and simultaneously a dissonant neighbor note.

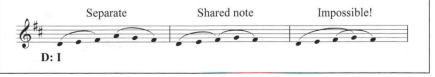

Separate   Shared note   Impossible!

D: I

other elaborations have their dissonant notes supported properly in the harmonic and contrapuntal structures of the music.

Harmonic analysis

Before outlining stage three in more detail, it is worth exploring the harmonic aspect of analysis more fully. Harmonic analysis in the foreground (stage one) should be familiar enough, but the way in which harmonies can be grouped together into larger units may be somewhat less so. Example 4.3 contains examples of the main types of harmonic unit, showing these groupings by means of slurs under the Roman numerals themselves. Marking harmonic units in this way forces you to be really clear about the harmonic implications of larger-scale linear patterns; when it comes to presenting the final version of your analysis, you will probably not want to include this level of detail, as the graph could get rather cluttered.

The first phrase of the chorale in Example 4.3 provides a simple example of I–V–I, in which the associated linear units are third progressions in the soprano and a neighbor note in the bass line.

The second phrase exemplifies the harmonic unit of I–V. The first three beats of the phrase, in the second measure of the example, show a common variant on I–V–I in which the dominant is replaced by VII, arriving on the dominant at the beginning of the next measure. The arrival on the dominant is further elaborated in an example of the V–V harmonic unit listed above.

The third phrase (starting three measures from the end) of Example 4.3 is an example of a progression between two third-related chords. Here, the third progression in soprano, tenor and bass all prolong the goal harmony of I.

There are four main types of harmonic unit that are most commonly found in tonal music, with examples of all four appearing in Example 4.3:

1   closed harmonic units of I–V–I and V–I, in which the primary harmony is the tonic;

2   open harmonic units of I–V. Although the goal harmony is usually primary, in the case of I–V a linear progression, for example, can elaborate either tonic or dominant, depending on the context. Progressions from I–V are marked by a slur that starts under the tonic and then curls up and over the dominant;

3   elaborations of the dominant (V–V);

4   third-related harmonies (e.g. VI and I), in which the final chord is primary.

Example 4.3 J. S. Bach, Chorale "Schaut, ihr Sünder" (Riemenschneider No. 171), slightly adapted

As with almost all linear progressions that span two chords, the first and last notes of the fourth progression in the second phrase of Example 4.3 are members of the goal harmony of V. The fifth progression in the bass of the same phrase, however, is the most common exception to this principle; although it fills in the space between tonic and dominant, its first and last notes correspond to the initial tonic harmony.

The final phrase sees a closed I–V–I bass arpeggiation preceded by a progression from V–I, this time in F major. The I–V–I is elaborated by the addition of chord II and a six-four decoration of the dominant. Just as the dominant in the first phrase provides harmonic support for the passing note, so the extra harmonies here support the passing notes of a fifth progression (B♭ is supported by II; A by the six-four and G by V).

The preceding discussion does not necessarily mean that harmonic units should be found first and then linear units found to fit them. The harmonic and the linear are mutually dependent and thus equally important—they need each other in order to make sense. The process is therefore one of trial and error, in which the analyst tries various linear and harmonic units that seem to make musical sense until a good solution is found.

Stage three (middleground analysis)

The basic principle of stage three is simple: identify larger-scale linear units in the middleground, ensuring that they make sense of corresponding harmonic units. In practice, this often means choosing a note from each foreground elaboration identified in stage two and then finding a way of linking these notes into a linear unit. Example 4.4 shows the stages one to three for a short extract from a Beethoven piano sonata. Unlike Example 4.1, this example is presented the usual way up, with the deepest layers at the top and the surface of the music at the bottom, reflecting Schenker's interest in the way the music is generated from the background rather than in the process of reduction from the foreground. The summary in the box outlines the main elements of stage three, which are then explored in more detail in the main text in relation to Example 4.4.

The stage one harmonic analysis (Example 4.4d) is straightforward—the music moves from the tonic to a dominant seventh in the fourth measure and back again. The process of preparing the score and finding foreground elaborations is slightly more complicated than in the previous example, however, because of the way in which both melody and accompaniment imply several voices.

The left hand is a compound melody that arpeggiates each chord in a repeated pattern, creating a bass line and several inner voices. In Example 4.4c this is simplified to the four-voice chords that are being elaborated. The right hand consists of a series of leaps and descending third progressions. Example 4.4c eliminates repeated figures, and marks both the leaps between voices and the third progressions with slurs. Unlike in the accompaniment, it is usually best not to reduce melodic figures to chords at this stage because it might limit options later in the analytical process.

When looking at the four groups of notes analyzed in Example 4.4c, we are attempting in stage three to find a connecting thread between them that makes sense of the harmonies. Example 4.4b shows one possibility: an interpretation of the whole passage as a rising third progression from D to F. This makes good sense of the larger harmonic unit of I–V–I, as both D and F are members of the primary tonic harmony. Another important feature of this reading is that the passing note E is supported both harmonically (by the dominant) and contrapuntally (by the A in the bass).

The solution in Example 4.4b is attractive because it both finds a simple stepwise connection from one note to the next and also spans the whole passage, but it is not the only possible interpretation. An alternative connecting thread would be that each figure has A in common, as shown by the dotted slurs in Example 4.5. This is nice and simple, but it does not do justice to this passage to interpret it as the embellishment of a single A, when there is so much going on in the upper register.

A final possibility, shown by the stems and beams in Example 4.5, would be to connect the F–G–F together into a neighbor note figure. One problem with this is that it goes against the rhythmic sense of the passage—the D–E–F interpretation shown in Example 4.4b appears on the first beat of each measure and lasts a quaver, whereas the Fs in the first three measures appear as semiquavers on the final beat of the measure. It is even harder to hear the E at the beginning of m. 4 as less important than the semiquaver G.

Stage three summary

- Identify larger-scale linear and harmonic units, bearing in mind the following considerations:

  - As one gets deeper beneath the surface of the music, Schenker suggests that melodic fluency becomes increasingly important. The contrapuntal lines should move mostly by step and be as simple and smooth as possible.
  - Linear patterns are most convincing when they have good contrapuntal and harmonic support (i.e. passing and neighbor notes should be made consonant by the bass line).
  - Decisions as to which notes are structurally more important should take account of melodic and metric prominence (i.e. you can take into account the prominence of notes according to their position in the texture and in the measure).

Notation

- Use stems and beams to show large-scale elaborations and label them clearly.
- Mark middleground elaborations using a combination of stems, flags and slurs as discussed in the following chapter.
- Use downward stems in the bass to mark the roots of principal supporting harmonies.
- Mark harmonic units with slurs beneath the Roman numerals and progressions from I–V with a slur that curls up and over the V. Approach chords to the dominant (e.g. II or IV) can be joined to V with a horizontal line—this is particularly helpful if the basic harmonic unit is V–I or V–V.
- Use slurs to connect the main arpeggiations in the bass (I–V, V–I) and also to mark elaborations of these notes.
- Use dotted slurs where necessary to show when two foreground linear units are elaborations of the same note (or of two notes an octave apart).
- Use beams, stems and diagonal lines to clarify features such as unfolding and voice exchange, which involve movement between different voices.
- Use dotted slurs or arrows to show register transfers.

A summary of notational conventions can be found on www.SchenkerGUIDE.com.

Example 4.4 Beethoven, Piano Sonata in D minor, Op. 31, No. 2, Allegretto

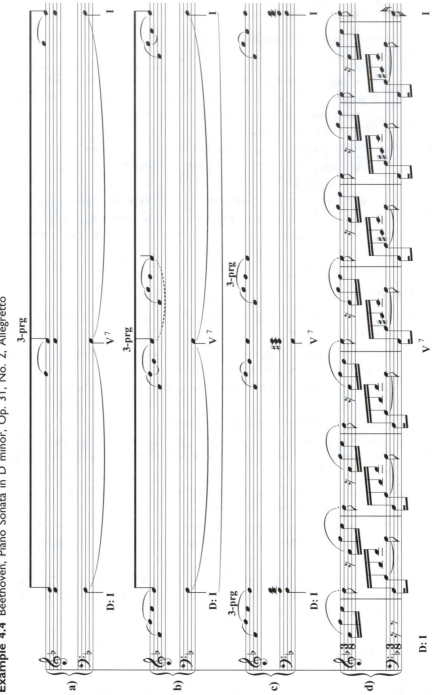

Example 4.6d shows stage two, and in this case none of the notes need to be omitted, as there are no consecutively repeated pitches or phrases. Four third progressions are identified as immediate elaborations of foreground harmonies, and the subdominant in the third measure also has an incomplete upper neighbor note that leads onto the D. In addition there are various minor skips between voices in the left hand.

Example 4.6 Mozart, *Nannerl's Notebook*, Menuet, KV 5

I have tried to keep things simple in Example 4.4b, but it could in fact be presented slightly more elegantly—the reason I have not done so is to show as clearly as possible the progression from one stage of the analysis to the next. The first figure (and the similar groupings that follow) would more properly be notated as an unfolding of the interval from A to D. The falling third progression is then understood as a reaching over that falls onto the D by step.

D: I

Example 4.5 Alternative analysis of Beethoven, Piano Sonata in D minor, Op. 31, No. 2

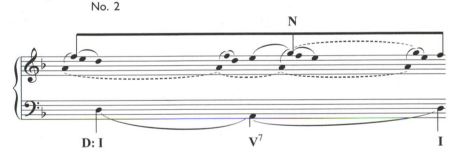

D: I   V^7 I

The A naturals at the beginning of each figure are easily explained as a lower voice, but the upper neighbor note shown in Example 4.5 is a little trickier, because it appears above the main voice of the ascending D–E–F. Schenker explains this sort of elaboration as a reaching over (see Chapter 2), in which a melody leaps upwards above the main voice and then descends back down onto it. There are two types of reaching over in this passage. The first is seen with the initial leap to F, which then descends via a passing note onto the principal voice represented by the D (the end of the fourth measure sees the same pattern up a tone). The second can be seen at the end of m. 3, in which the F descends by step onto the E in the next measure and is decorated by a brief leap back down to D—the G at the end of the

The graph in Example 4.4a leaves out quite a lot of a foreground detail, which is normal practice in middleground graphs. The advantage is that it is much easier to see what is going on without all the clutter of the foreground. The disadvantage is that it takes slightly more effort to relate it back to the surface of the music. It is a good discipline to analyze all the notes methodically as suggested in the four-stage method, but, as discussed in Chapter 5, the successful presentation of Schenkerian graphs is partly a matter of getting the right balance between what stays in and what is left out.

passage leads onto F in the same way. This second type is the more significant one here because, as can clearly be seen in Example 4.4a, these two reaching-over figures introduce the next note of the rising third progression in each case.

Stage four (background analysis)

The procedure for stage four is the same as for the previous stage, the difference being that one is looking for much more specific patterns—the various elaborations of the *Ursatz*. These basic patterns were introduced in the previous chapter.

In a nutshell, the aim of background analysis is to show how a piece can be understood as single, unified prolongation of the tonic that begins on $\hat{3}$ (i.e. scale degree 3), $\hat{5}$ or $\hat{8}$ and descends stepwise to finish $\hat{2}$–$\hat{1}$. The whole structure is supported by some elaboration of I–V–I. The deep level elaborations of the *Ursatz* tend to correspond in some way to major formal divisions of a piece (e.g. Exposition and Recapitulation or Minuet and Trio). If you presume from the outset that some form of the *Ursatz* will emerge in the background, this inevitably affects earlier decisions. The patterns that inform stage four, in other words, also guide the layer analysis of stage three.

In order for a background analysis to be convincing, it is important that there is a clear descent to $\hat{1}$. Sometimes an *Urlinie* descent can span a very long section of music, with each note considerably prolonged, but it is a mistake to look only for this sort of very protracted descent. It is also quite common for the final descent to occur relatively late and quickly.

Example 4.6 shows the various stages of analysis from foreground to background in a short extract from a Mozart minuet. Stage one at the bottom of the example has only two very minor complications. At the end of the third measure, the figured bass shows a second inversion chord leading onto the dominant in a classic example of the cadential six-four (see Chapter 2). The first two beats of the second measure are not a straightforward

Stage four summary

- Identify a convincing *Urlinie* descent and *Bassbrechung*:
  - The *Urlinie* must descend diatonically to $\hat{1}$ by step from one of three possible *Kopftone* (head tones): $\hat{3}$, $\hat{5}$ or $\hat{8}$.
  - Once a scale degree of the *Urlinie* is established, the descent can only continue down—it cannot return to previous scale degrees (although this does not mean that $\hat{3}$ or $\hat{5}$, for example, cannot be elaborated by a large-scale neighbor note). The exception is the interruption, which can occur only after $\hat{2}$ and always returns to the original *Kopfton*.
  - For an *Urlinie* from $\hat{5}$ or $\hat{8}$ to be convincing each note of the descent must be properly supported harmonically and contrapuntally.
- Explore the possibility of standard elaborations of the *Ursatz* in the first-level middleground (i.e. directly prolonging the notes of the *Urlinie* and *Bassbrechung*), such as initial ascent or interruption. These are detailed in Chapter 3.

Notation

- The *Urlinie* is marked with upwards stems and beams and each note of the descent is labeled according to which degree of the scale it represents in relation to the home key—these scale degrees are marked with a caret (^) so that they can clearly be distinguished from other numbers on the score.
- The *Bassbrechung* (I–V–I) is marked with downwards stems and beams connecting the root notes of these chords.
- Interruptions are marked with a double slash after the $\hat{2}$.
- Elaborations involving changes of register can be clarified with arrows and dotted slurs.
- Elaborations involving changes of voice can be clarified with stems, beams and arrows as appropriate.

dominant chord either. The first beat has the fifth of the chord in the bass against the tonic, but taken together with the second beat the harmony is clearly a dominant seventh. Thinking ahead to the next stage of the analysis is worthwhile if the harmony seems at all ambiguous—these first two beats of the second measure simply skip from an upper to a lower voice within the chord of V.

As shown in Example 4.6c (stage three), the identification of the harmonic units of V–I in the second measure and at the end allows the ungrouped notes from the previous stage to be understood as descending third progressions that elaborate the tonic. Note how the IV is linked in m. 3 as an approach chord to the dominant.

The I–VII–I in the first measure is also grouped together as a harmonic unit, which presents a choice as to whether the triplets are an elaboration of a larger-scale third progression starting on F or A. Melodically, the A–B♭–C is more prominent as the upper voice, but metrically the F–G–A is more accentuated. The upper voice is the simpler choice, as Example 4.6b shows, because the first measure is then a series of rising parallel thirds decorated by triplets. As shown in Example 4.6a, choosing the lower voice means interpreting the triplets as reaching-over figures—the melody reaches over to the upper voice A as a means of dropping back down onto the G and then to the B♭ in order to drop onto A. This decision also has a knock-on effect on the next measure, in which there is a choice between C and A.

From the point of view of stage three layer analysis, there is not much to choose between these two interpretations; it is therefore time to move on to stage four of the analysis and consider what form of the *Urlinie* the passage might elaborate. As shown in Example 4.6b, choosing the upper voice suggests an interpretation of the passage as a descent from $\hat{5}$ to $\hat{1}$, whereas opting for the lower voice suggests a descent from $\hat{3}$ (Example 4.6a).

In order to make an *Urlinie* from $\hat{5}$ meaningful, it is necessary to find a clear descent in which each note has contrapuntal and harmonic support. The B♭ in the top voice in m. 3 is a good candidate for $\hat{4}$ (the first step of the descent) because it is supported by IV, which moves by step to the dominant. If, on the other hand, the extract elaborates a descent from $\hat{3}$, this B♭ in the top voice would be interpreted instead as a neighbor note.

In Example 4.6c, the A at the end of the penultimate measure is shown as the beginning of a third progression that elaborates the tonic over a V–I harmonic unit. If the background is interpreted as a descent from $\hat{5}$, then this A becomes a passing note onto the final $\hat{2}$ of the descent. In terms of the descent from $\hat{3}$, however, we have already had $\hat{3}$ in the first measure, so its fleeting return here after the B♭ neighbor note is not so structurally important, which makes sense in that a cadential six-four is only a passing harmony on the way to the dominant. There is some disagreement among Schenkerian analysts as to whether a cadential six-four is sufficient support for $\hat{3}$ in this context. There is no doubt that it is weak, but this does not seem to me to be a good enough reason to discount the viability of such structures.

Making a final decision in the slightly artificial circumstances of such a short extract is not really possible, but I find the descent from $\hat{3}$ slightly more persuasive, mostly because of the way in which $\hat{5}$ is approached in the first measure. The B♭ that precedes it is the diminished fifth of chord VII

Some analysts (notably Allen Forte) argue that a descent from $\hat{5}$ is only convincing if it is approached via $\sharp\hat{4}$. In this case, then, the B♭ passing note at the beginning of Example 4.6b would have to be natural, which would imply a tonicization of V (a brief modulation into C major). This does not have to be a binding condition, but it is worth bearing in mind when deciding whether a piece may be better explained as a descent from $\hat{5}$ or $\hat{3}$. In a passage only four measures long, this is not really an issue—there is no space for a tonicization of V in any case.

and as such it is more convincing as a resolution down onto A as $\hat{3}$, than as part of an ascent to V.

The analytical process at stage four thus involves the balancing of several considerations. Although the same basic principles of melodic and contrapuntal fluency from stage three still hold, the analyst also has to take account of Schenker's proposed models of *Ursatz* elaboration, including such factors as the requirement for a properly supported descent. In a longer piece, as discussed in Chapter 3, traditional ideas of musical form can also affect our view of where the major divisions in the Schenkerian structure might arise. Although the analysis is at all levels shaped by Schenker's quite restrictive framework, there is still plenty of room for interpretation.

In both versions of the analysis, the first measure comprises a rising figure to the *Kopfton* ($\hat{3}$ or $\hat{5}$) that Schenker calls an initial ascent. The whole passage is therefore the elaboration of an arch in which a tension is introduced by this initial ascent to the *Kopfton* at the end of the first measure, and then resolved through a descent to $\hat{1}$. Although this passage is rather short to show how this sort of musical tension works on the large scale, the principle is the same whether a piece of music spans only a few measures or several hundred.

A final worked example

The final example of this chapter works through an analysis of the first half of a Mozart minuet. Example 4.7c shows the first two stages, in which the rhythmic notation is removed before analyzing the foreground. There are not any literally repeated notes to remove, but the left hand consists of a repeated unfolding of a fairly mobile lower voice and an upper voice that stays on C for the first five measures. Example 4.7c simplifies this by showing the first two notes as a chord and then repeating the inner voice C at the beginning of the next main phrase. It would clutter up the analysis to show each pair of quavers as an unfolding or to keep repeating the C in an inner

Example 4.7 Mozart, *Eight Minuets*, KV 315, No. 1, Trio

voice. Strictly speaking this sort of decision belongs to the next stage, but, as with all stages of analysis, it pays to look ahead.

The foreground analysis is reasonably straightforward, with a series of alternating tonic and dominant cadences culminating in a cadential II–V–I at the end. Most of the decorations, as shown in Example 4.7c are ascending and descending third progressions, the only other being an unfolding of a sixth from C to A at the beginning, which is repeated in the upbeat to the fifth measure.

Example 4.7b shows stage three, in which an attempt is made to join things up into larger units. From a harmonic point of view there is not much choice—the piece clearly consists of a series of I–V–I units, the last elaborated with a II approach to the dominant. Note the way in which both the harmonic units and elaborations can involve overlapping the last element of one with the first of the next; the I at the beginning of m. 3, for example, is part of both I–V–I units. As is often the case, the descending third progression that begins the extract is best interpreted as an unfolding of a two-note chord containing A and F—the third progression fills in the gap of this unfolding with stepwise motion. Looking at the bass line as well, however, it is clear that this is actually a voice exchange, because this unfolds the same interval the other way around (from F to A). The third measure reverses this voice exchange and the fifth repeats it.

The upper part in the m. 2 is also an unfolding, this time from C to E, the bottom note of which is shown in brackets to show that it connects back to the C from the opening. The E therefore forms a lower neighbor note with the surrounding Fs, which is counterpointed against an upper neighbor in the left hand. The Bb in m. 4 similarly forms a neighbor note with the surrounding A naturals.

The final two measures are interpreted here as a G neighbor note to the two Fs, but if we are going to look for an *Ursatz* in this extract as if it were a whole piece, the final G to F will have to be rethought so that they complete a $\hat{2}$–$\hat{1}$ descent.

Example 4.7a shows how the whole passage can be understood as an elaboration of $\hat{3}$ involving four main voices. If the opening is basically a two note chord in the top two voices, the lower of these two voices (F) is the first to be elaborated (by the E neighbor) after which the upper of the two voices (A) becomes the focus. The dotted slurs on Example 4.7a show how the top voice at the beginning does not literally continue to be prolonged over the first two measures but is picked up again at the end of the third. The left hand works in the same way and both hands suggest a further middle part—the Cs shown in brackets—which continues to be hinted at throughout the passage.

At the conclusion of this long elaboration of $\hat{3}$ (the beginning of m. 7) there is a descent from $\hat{2}$ to $\hat{1}$. This passage is interesting in that it turns out to spend nearly the whole phrase moving around within the space of the chord outlined by the A in the top voice and the F in the bass right at the beginning.

Example 4.7a could probably be presented in a more economical way; it may be that some the inner voice details, for example, can be removed. On the other hand, depending on what the graph is designed to show, all six voices could be left in but some of their decorations pared down a little. The next chapter discusses different ways of presenting your analytical findings, while the rest of this handbook takes a look at some longer pieces of music in order to explore some of the issues about which a Schenkerian analysis might be concerned.

Chapter 5

Presenting a Schenkerian analysis

The four stages outlined in Chapter 4 set out a step-by-step method; the resulting graphs should be understood as work in progress rather than an end in themselves. This chapter therefore explores how to present analytical work, clarifying and refining the notation already introduced. Most published Schenkerian analyses explore music on a variety of levels of detail; what follows concerns the practicalities of presenting different types of graph. If these discussions stray beyond matters strictly concerned with presentation, that is because notational convention in Schenkerian analysis is inextricably linked with the view of musical structure that it portrays.

As outlined in previous chapters there are three basic levels of detail that a Schenkerian analysis might show. Schenker refers to his most detailed graphs as foreground or *Urlinie-tafel* (lit. original line table). Such analyses show the relationship between the foreground detail and as much middleground and background as can practically be included, and, as is common practice, I shall refer to the first of them as *foreground* graphs. Because they analyze nearly every note of the original music, it is relatively rare to find whole pieces represented through foreground graphs in published analyses, unless the piece in question is very short.

Analyses that exclude the foreground detail are usually referred to as *middleground* graphs. In his *Five Graphic Analyses* (Schenker 1969) Schenker includes several numbered middleground layers (*Schichten*) that show successively more detail as the analysis moves from the *Ursatz* to the foreground. I use the term *middleground* specifically to refer to graphs that consistently show the same level of detail throughout. I will make a distinction between middleground graphs that systematically present a particular layer of a piece of music and *middleground summaries*, which offer an overview of the whole piece, along with any particularly notable features of the middleground. Such graphs are often referred to as the background, but, strictly speaking, anything other than the notes of the *Ursatz* itself is actually part of the middleground (including such features as initial ascent, interruption etc.). The terms foreground, middleground and background are used quite informally by analysts; the purpose of defining three distinct types of graph in this chapter is simply to set out the various presentational options as clearly as possible.

Foreground graphs

There are no musical features in Example 5.1 that have not been introduced already, but the analysis is here presented more elegantly. What defines this as a foreground graph is the inclusion of surface detail, not the absence of middleground or background; a foreground graph is an analysis of the surface of the music, but usually it will also indicate how this relates to deeper layers.

The most obvious difference from the graphs of the previous chapter is that harmonic units are not shown beneath the Roman numerals. Although it is very helpful to have harmonic units marked when you are working on an analysis, there is a danger of cluttering up your finished graph with duplicated information. When analysis is still in progress, marking harmonic units ensures that you do not end up with linear elaborations that contradict the tonal structure of the music; with a finished graph, however, the harmonic units can relatively easily be inferred from other markings. In the first three measures, for example, it is clear from the neighbor note in the upper voice that the harmonic unit is I–V–I.

The neighbor note near the beginning of the extract is highlighted by a combination of stems and slurs. The stems distinguish the members of the neighbor note figure from its surrounding decorations, while the slur (along with optional label) clarifies where it begins and ends. The other main method of indicating middleground elaborations is used to show the third progression in the next three measures: the stems of the rising third progression are connected by a beam. Both notations mean essentially the same thing, but stems and beams become increasingly useful in more complex music, because they are a clear way of marking out structurally important notes from their elaborations. Another way of clarifying a figure is to use a flagged stem, as with the neighbor note in the sixth measure.

Notice how the harmonies in the fourth and fifth measures of Example 5.1 are notated. F major is elaborated by its dominant (C), and this is marked by showing how these two chords are I and V of III. The bracket clarifies which chords belong to this brief tonicization.

Example 5.1 Corelli, Violin Sonata, Op. 5, No. 12, Adagio, mm. 1–16, foreground graph

The surface decorations in Example 5.1 are shown with unstemmed note heads, such as the incomplete upper neighbor E in the first bar and the complete neighbor-note figure in the third. Their relationship to the middle-ground figures that underpin them is shown by slurs. If you include a note in an analytical graph, it must be grouped with something by slurs or stems and beams; the whole point of a Schenkerian analysis is to show relationships between notes.

Melodic elaborations in the bass should be marked in the same way as those in the top line, but it is additionally important that harmonic and contrapuntal support of the elaborations in the top line is highlighted with downward stems. Much of the bass line of this fairly simple Corelli extract consists of the roots of the chords, and in such cases slurs are used to connect tonics and dominants as well as for showing the linear connections such as the way the B♭ acts as a neighbor note to A in mm. 7–8.

It is important when preparing a Schenkerian graph to think through the implications of all the analytical notation that you employ. The following series of graphs, which analyze extracts from the Corelli in Example 5.1, outline some notational problems that are sometimes found in student work.

One common problem is a tendency to connect one note to the next in the foreground with a series of slurs, as in Example 5.2a. Connecting a sequence of notes in this way tells us nothing more about the music than the fact that one note follows the next. The slurs in mm. 3–4 could mean that the C is a neighbor note to the D or vice versa, or that the C is the beginning of a third progression—it is simply impossible to tell. Every time you draw a slur you should ask yourself to what harmony the group of notes belongs. In mm. 3–4 a longer slur connecting the two Ds would clearly show how the C forms part of a complete neighbor note figure—single slurs should only be used where there are genuinely only two notes involved in a prolongation, as in the neighbor note E in the first measure.

Where one middleground elaboration runs into the next, as in the first six measures of the Corelli, it is important to distinguish between them. Whereas the third progression in Example 5.1 is clearly set apart from the surrounding neighbor notes, the continuous beam used in Example 5.2b is much more difficult to interpret. It is also important to remember that, while prolongations may share a first and last note, they must not overlap. The notation of the Example 5.2c suggests an impossible structure—the C♯ in m. 2 cannot be a dissonant neighbor note to the following D and at the same time the consonant beginning of a third progression. There are other

Example 5.2 Examples of poor foreground notation: (a) Meaningless slurs; (b) Meaningless beams; (c) Overlapping elaborations

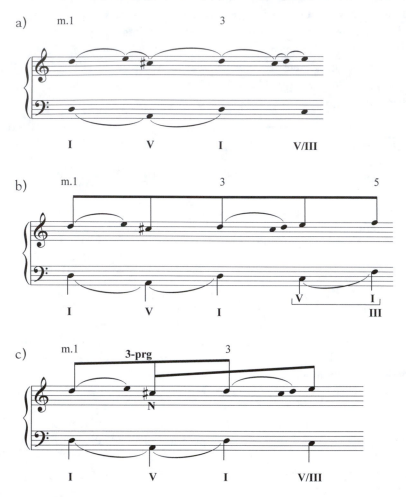

problems with Example 5.2c, in particular the fact that the third progression does not prolong a coherent harmonic unit.

As in most of the analyses in this book, Example 5.1 is aligned with the original music for the sake of clarity. This is not, however, a normal feature of foreground analyses; usually the reader is expected to have a score of the piece in front of them. It is therefore important that measure numbers are clearly and frequently marked so that your reader can quickly and easily find the music to which the analysis refers.

Example 5.3, from the beginning of the Corelli, highlights an issue that is somewhere in between analysis and its presentation. The E at the end of the first measure is shown as a neighbor note to the D, because it appears while the tonic harmony is still in force. An alternative analysis would be to understand this E as an anticipation of the next harmony (the dominant) and, from a linear perspective, it would involve a skip to the lower voice of C♯. Generally speaking, it is better to keep the foreground analysis simple— if a note is not part of a harmony, then analyze it accordingly. Schenkerian analysts do not invariably keep to this rule, but there are good reasons for doing so. In the case of Example 5.3, marking the E as a part of the next harmony would open up the possibility during middleground analysis of selecting it as a structural note that is prolonged by C♯, a somewhat counter-intuitive analysis given what is actually happening on the surface of the music. A Schenkerian graph already entails so many subjective interpretations at deeper layers of the structure that it is better to found these decisions on as logical an analysis of the foreground as possible.

The scope for subjective interpretation in middleground analysis is demonstrated by the alternative analyses of mm. 6–8 in Example 5.4. Example 5.4b shows a more immediately logical reading of these three measures than that presented in Example 5.1. In Example 5.4b, the E at the end of m. 6 and the C♯ at the beginning of m. 8 are shown as neighbor notes to the D at the beginning of m. 7. As one would expect the two dominant harmonies

Example 5.3 Corelli, Violin Sonata, Op. 5, No. 12, Adagio, mm. 1–2, foreground graph

to be subordinate to the tonic, this analysis makes good sense. In an inversion of this reading, however, Example 5.4c (like Example 5.1) implies that the tonic in m. 7 is subordinate to the dominants on either side; the tonic is presented as harmonic support for the D passing note in the context of a dominant prolongation. Note that I have reinstated the slurs beneath the Roman numerals in this example—it is precisely when making such analytical decisions that it is helpful to have a clear and graphic representation of the harmonic consequences.

The middleground analyses at the end of Examples 5.4b and 5.4c show how these different interpretations might impact upon our reading of the first eight measures. The analysis in Example 5.4b results in the tonic chord at the beginning of m. 7 being interpreted as the end of an elaboration of I from the beginning of the piece. From a linear perspective, this suggests

Example 5.4 Corelli, Sonata for Violin, Op. 5, No. 12, Adagio, mm. 6–8; alternative foreground readings with their middleground consequences

that the structural melodic note being elaborated in the first seven measures is D, which then moves stepwise to C♯ in the final measure of the phrase.

While this is logical, it goes against the way I actually hear this phrase in two main ways: first, the F in m. 5 feels like the high point of the phrase—something that is poorly reflected in Example 5.4b; second, the tonic chord at the beginning of m. 7 does not sound to me like the end point of a linear-harmonic unit. This is partly to do with the fact that the tonic only lasts for one beat before moving straight to the subdominant, and partly because there seems to be a harmonic and linear momentum towards the cadence. I prefer the analysis in Example 5.4c because it more closely represents my subjective interpretation of the phrase. This is a good example of the constant negotiation in Schenkerian analysis between logic and methodological consistency on the one hand and musical and analytical intuition on the other. The need for this sort of negotiation can be seen either as a problem or as an opportunity to discover those aspects of a piece that are most open to interpretation. The difficulty in analyzing this phrase reflects the fact that this D minor tonic chord feels like a transitory moment on the way to the dominant.

A further reason for preferring the interpretation in Example 5.4c might be that it more easily fits the pattern of an *Urlinie* descending from $\hat{3}$ or $\hat{5}$ —something that is not really a possibility if we interpret this phrase as in Example 5.4b. If the corresponding part of the second phrase is interpreted in a similar way—the E in m. 14 would be a neighbor note to F at the end of the measure—it is almost impossible to find a convincing final descent through $\hat{2}$ to $\hat{1}$. In this Corelli movement there are other compelling reasons to interpret the music in this way, but looking forward to the background analysis of stage four also has an impact.

Middleground graphs

Middleground graphs remove some of the foreground detail in order to make the overall shape of the music easier to apprehend. Example 5.5 is aligned with the score for the purposes of clarity, but because part of the point of a middleground graph is its economy it is very rare to find the actual music included in this way. Most middleground graphs show two or three different layers at the same time. The elaborations in the layer closest to the foreground are shown as stemless notes with slurs. The neighbor note figure over the first three measures (D–C♯–D), for example, is decorated on the surface of the music by its own neighbor notes, which in the foreground graph in Example 5.1 were marked with slurs. Now that this surface detail has been removed, the middleground neighbor note is the elaboration closest to the surface and can therefore be marked with a slur. This means that larger-scale elaborations can now be marked with stems and beams without cluttering up the analysis. This method of showing two layers can be extended to cover

Example 5.5 Corelli, Violin Sonata, Op. 5, No. 12, Adagio, mm. 1–16, stage four analysis

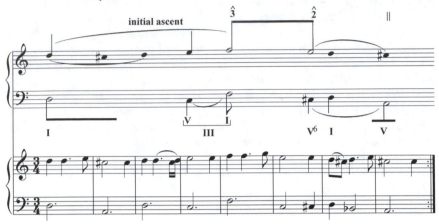

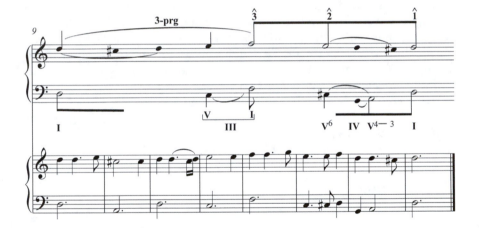

Incipit

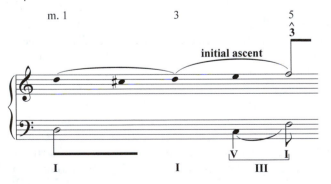

very large spans of music, with prolongations closer to the surface of the music slurred and those further from the surface beamed. Middleground graphs often show in addition how these two layers relate to the even deeper layer of the *Ursatz*. In this short Corelli piece the whole background structure is apparent, but a middleground graph of a longer movement might well show only an extract, in which case only part of the *Ursatz* will be shown.

The notation of the middleground should link the music up into units that span as large a section of music as possible. The presentation of the first five measures in Example 5.5 is thus better than that in the incipit. Both analyses are essentially the same in that they show a neighbor note followed by an ascending third progression. The difference is that Example 5.5 highlights the fact that the neighbor note is a prolongation of the same note as the third progression. The neighbor note is shown as a decoration of the first note of the third progression, which in turn shows much more clearly how the first five measures can be understood as a single linear motion from D to F.

The relatively restricted number of possible forms of the *Ursatz* means that the notation of this part of the analysis is the most prescriptive. The *Urlinie* is marked with caretted numbers representing scale degrees in relation to the tonic, and with stems and thick beams. In addition, open note heads (i.e. half notes) are used to represent the main notes of the descent. This notation should only be used to show the overall *Ursatz* structure in one of the forms prescribed by Schenker and outlined in Chapter 6. It is sometimes appropriate in longer pieces, however, to show how *Urlinie*-like descents are replicated in the middleground either in the tonic or as part of a tonicization— in such cases, the caretted numbers should be in brackets and the connecting beams less thick. The first-level middleground prolongation of the *Urlinie* is in this case the interruption. The point of interruption after the $\hat{2}$ is marked by the double slash at the end of the first phrase.

Like the *Urlinie*, the *Bassbrechung* also has its own distinctive notation so that the overall shape of the piece can quickly be seen from the analysis. Downward stems and thick beams along with open note heads are used to mark the tonics and dominants that support the descending notes of the *Urlinie*. The first five measures of Example 5.5 demonstrate the importance of this notation. By the time the initial ascent arrives on $\hat{3}$, that harmony has changed from I to III. From a Schenkerian perspective, the $\hat{3}$ belongs with the opening tonic on the deepest level, with the III being an elaboration closer to the surface. Similarly the $\hat{2}$ in m. 6 is aligned on the level of the *Ursatz* with the arrival on the root of the dominant at the end of the phrase two measures later—the first inversion is not nearly as emphatic as a structural dominant.

Schenker suggests that the overall shape of the bass can be understood as a series of scale steps in between the initial tonic and the final structural dominant. The overarching shape of this background bass prolongation is shown using open note heads with flagged stems. This notation can be seen on the F in m. 5 (and its counterpart in m.14), which shows that this Corelli movement has a bass pattern that moves twice from I through scale-step III to V before finally returning to the tonic at the end.[1]

Example 5.6 demonstrates an alternative *Ursatz* reading that is deliberately counter-intuitive in order to highlight some common problems in presenting background analyses. The first thing to check when evaluating whether an *Ursatz* is plausible is that the notes of the *Urlinie* make sense in terms of the harmonies with which they coincide. This is particularly problematic for the placement of Î in m. 15. Although the D is consonant with the subdominant chord on the first beat, it swiftly becomes a suspended fourth over the dominant for which the first beat is clearly a preparation. It does not seem plausible to suggest that the tension-releasing final arrival on Î

Example 5.6 Problematic reading of Corelli, Violin Sonata, Op. 5, No. 12

occurs in this harmonic context. The harmonic support for $\hat{2}$ does not seem too convincing either, but this is bound up in a wider interpretational problem as outlined below.

A key question for assessing the plausibility of background descents is whether the material in between the notes of the *Urlinie* can reasonably be understood as an elaboration of either the preceding or succeeding scale degree. From this perspective, there are several problems with the placement of $\hat{2}$ on Example 5.6. The first is that the C major harmony in m. 12—the dominant of chord III—is the least structurally significant harmony of the whole phrase; it seems highly unlikely that the surrounding harmonies are somehow going to be an elaboration of this chord. The third progression starting in m. 8 is not grammatical, in that A major and C major harmonies, although a third apart, do not share two notes and, furthermore, the progression from C♯ to E cannot be understood as a decoration of C major in any case. The analysis could be made slightly more convincing by showing the C♯ in m. 8 as a neighbor note to the D in mm. 7 and 9 and thus as a continued prolongation of $\hat{1}$, but we would still be left with the same problem from mm. 12–14. Even without this problem there is still an issue of consistency. The F naturals in mm. 5 and 13 appear in an almost identical context so it seems counter-intuitive to analyze it as a goal of a third progression the first time but merely as a neighbor note the second time. Musical features can of course change their context, but there seems no good reason to treat these two F naturals differently in this case.

The initial $\hat{3}$ is the least problematic of the *Urlinie* notes in Example 5.6 in that it makes harmonic sense of its surroundings. However this analysis entails positing that the linear-harmonic structure does not coincide with the basic binary structure of the movement, which divides at the imperfect cadence at m. 8. Although Schenker views such divisions as a surface feature secondary to the deeper logic of the *Ursatz*, he nevertheless takes more account of them than he sometimes admits—his analyses virtually never cut across major formal divisions.[2] The ultimate criterion for evaluating an *Urlinie* analysis is the extent to which it is plausible. Any judgment of plausibility has to balance a wide range of factors from foreground harmony through wider linear-harmonic interpretation through to musical intuition.

Systematic middleground graphs of the type shown in Example 5.5 and Example 5.6 are ideal for explorations of the shape and trajectory of a piece and of the way in which such middleground details—the real heart of any Schenkerian analysis—can be reconciled with Schenker's background archetypes. With longer works, however, this systematic attention to a particular layer of the structure can still generate more detail than is conducive to showing clearly a particular aspect of the deep structure, which is where the final type of graph outlined in this chapter comes into its own.

Middleground summaries

Many of Schenker's own analyses show the background structure plus a summary of any particularly significant middleground or even foreground features.
These middleground summaries present the most notable characteristics,
offering an overview that aims to give an understanding of the work in
question as a whole. The main difference from middleground graphs is that
a middleground summary does not attempt to show systematically the same
level of detail throughout the analysis.

If a middleground graph is good at showing the detailed shape of a piece,
a graph such as that in Example 5.7 is aimed rather at demonstrating
Schenker's maxim "always the same but not in the same way." We can see
at a glance how the general outline of the piece conforms to the archetypal
Ursatz pattern of an interrupted descent from $\hat{3}$; at the same time the most
distinctive feature of the movement's structure is also clearly shown—the
proportionately long initial ascent accompanied by a tonicization of $\hat{3}$. Notice
that the graph does not show the equivalent initial ascent that precedes
the $\hat{3}$ in m. 9, because this repetition of material would be immediately
obvious to anyone comparing the graph with the score. Example 5.7 similarly
excludes any prolongation of the descent itself, because there is nothing
particularly unusual or notable about the middleground or foreground at this
point. Such details are excluded so that the graph is as uncluttered as
possible and so that it easily fits onto one system. It is often useful to include

Example 5.7 Corelli, Violin Sonata, Op. 5, No. 12, Adagio, middleground summary

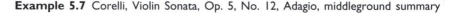
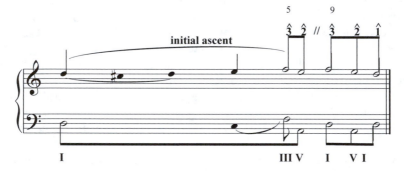

Incipit A: mm.3–5

this type of middleground summary at the beginning of an analytical study so that readers can locate subsequent detailed discussions of particular passages within this wider context. You will usually expect a reader to have a score to hand when looking at your analyses, but it can sometimes be helpful to bring a middleground analysis to life by making use of incipits. In this graph, the incipit reminds the reader at a glance how the music arrives on the *Kopfton* of $\hat{3}$ in m. 5.

Schenker's emphasis on counterpoint means that, in the deep layers in particular, he avoids parallel fifths and octaves. Although there may in fact be parallel motion to octaves or fifths in some middleground layers, the convention is to include enough detail that the appearance of such motion

Example 5.8 Corelli, Violin Sonata, Op. 5, No. 12, Adagio, mm. 1–5, alternative middleground summaries

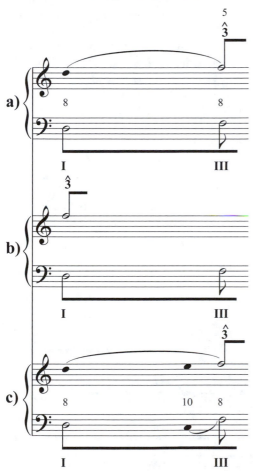

is avoided. Schenker argues that because apparent middleground parallel fifths or octaves are disguised by the way they are elaborated, it would give a misleading impression to produce middleground graphs full of this type of motion. The implicit parallel octaves in the first five measures of the first level middleground of the Corelli are shown in Example 5.8a. It is usual practice either to reduce the level of detail (Example 5.8b) or increase it (Example 5.8c) in order to eliminate the appearance of octaves.

Schenkerian notation in practice

There are many different ways of notating a Schenkerian analysis; even within Schenker's own work, which was published over a period of thirty years, there is a lack of consistency. Although the basic principles remain the same, scholars tend to find their own solutions to notational problems. Although you should not find mainstream Schenkerian graphs too difficult to read, you will need to learn to be flexible in how you understand even the most basic notational features.

If you want to become fluent in understanding the broad range of notational conventions, you need to spend some time looking at graphs that have heavily influenced subsequent scholars. One very important source is obviously Schenker's *Free Composition* (Schenker 1977), from which Example 5.9 is taken. Apart from the whole analysis being crammed onto one staff to save space, most of the notation should be familiar enough in this reasonably straightforward middleground summary.

Notice how Schenker notates the final I–V–I in the bass line using upward stems and beams and filled note heads. This is to reflect Schenker's understanding of the *Ursatz* as a single descent, of which the interruption structure here is a prolongation. The notation shows that the second I–V is structurally less significant—an elaboration of the final tonic. For the

Example 5.9 Mozart, Piano Sonata in C Major, K. 545, first movement, from Schenker's *Free Composition*

Source: Schenker 1977: Figure 47/1

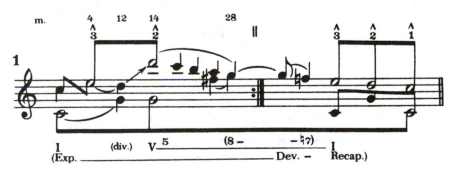

Apart from the interruption, the most notable features of the prolongation
of the *Ursatz* in Example 5.9 is the register transfer at m. 14, which is
highlighted by an ascending arrow. This transfer and the ensuing descending
fifth correspond to the beginning of the second subject. As is often the case,
Schenker does not show this material in the recapitulation, partly because
there is no need to duplicate this part of the analysis.

same reason, Schenker sometimes shows the second $\hat{3}$–$\hat{2}$ of an interruption
as structurally less important. Although this notation is recommended towards
the beginning of *Free Composition*, Schenker himself frequently stems all
the *Urlinie* notes as suggested in this book, presumably because this makes
it much easier to see the overall structure on the graph.

Example 5.10 is a rather different type of graph from *Free Composition*,
showing part of the second subject from a Beethoven sonata's last movement.
The middleground graph demonstrates how the passage can be understood
as a prolongation of $\hat{2}$ in the dominant minor (G♯—the home key is C♯
minor). Schenker shows how the extract is basically an elaboration of V,
recognizing the tonicization of this chord by analyzing the harmonies in
relation to the dominant.

It is quite common to find *Ursatz* prolongations replicated on a small
scale as the basis for a phrase of section of music. In this case a descent
from $\hat{5}$ over a prolongation of I–V–I underpins part of the second subject.
This "local" *Urlinie* is labeled with careted numbers that relate to the scale
degrees of the dominant in brackets. The $\hat{2}$ of the tonic becomes $\hat{5}$ in the
dominant and descends to $\hat{1}$.

A local *Ursatz* form in the middle of a piece can be subject to all the
various prolongations and variants associated with it. In this extract, the $\hat{3}$

Example 5.10 Beethoven, Piano Sonata, Op. 27, No. 2, third movement, mm. 25–37,
from Schenker's *Free Composition*

Source: Schenker 1977: Figure 104/1

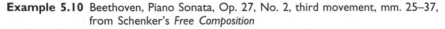
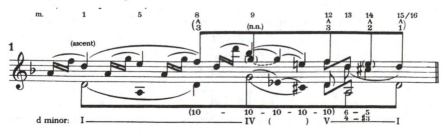

of the descent is not actually present in the music, so Schenker shows it in brackets over the note that substitutes for it (a C). A very good way of improving your understanding is to relate such graphs to the music and to try and work out why Schenker analyzes the music in the way that he does.

Another Schenker volume that repays careful study from the point of view of notation is his *Five Graphic Analyses* (Schenker 1969). This book contains comprehensive graphs on multiple levels without any explanatory text, and probably represents Schenker's most carefully notated mature work. The analysis of Bach's C Major Prelude from this collection is probably the most widely reproduced of Schenker's graphs.

A third key text—Felix Salzer's *Structural Hearing*—has been particularly influential on North American analysts, and if you want to understand the origins of some otherwise rather mysterious notational conventions, this is a good place to start.[3] Salzer's book introduces some fundamental changes to both the theory and practice of Schenkerian analysis in order to broaden the range of repertoire that might be tackled, both forward into the twentieth century and back into the fourteenth century. Example 5.11 displays some features that have had a considerable influence on analytical notation. Unlike in Schenker's mature analyses Salzer is frequently happy to leave notes unaccounted for on his graphs. His presentation of harmonic structure on the other hand is very clear. Although his use of multiple levels of Roman numerals will be familiar from this book, the graph in Example 5.11 also contains some novel notational features. "Em," for example, in the second measure is an abbreviation of "embellishing chord," one of several structural features that are distinctly Salzerian rather than Schenkerian.

A final text that is worth studying, again because of its historic importance as a textbook, is Allen Forte and Stephen Gilbert's *Introduction to Schenkerian Analysis* (Forte and Gilbert 1982). Although you will find their graphs reasonably similar to those in the present volume, their style of presentation is very distinctive. If Salzer's graphs are often rather sparse in their use of slurs and beams, Forte and Gilbert's show vast numbers of multiple connections between notes. Example 5.12 shows a foreground and middleground graph from the third movement of Beethoven's Op. 109 piano sonata. Where Salzer would use stems of various heights, Forte and Gilbert here use beams at different levels. In the first half of the theme, beams are used to show the $\hat{3}$ of the *Urlinie* being prolonged by a descending fourth progression, the second note of which is elaborated by a rising third progression. Another feature of many of Forte and Gilbert's analyses is their interest in motivic parallels. In the first of the graphs of Example 5.12, the brackets show where motifs involving G♯ and B appear. A Schenkerian approach to motivic analysis is discussed in Chapter 9. The more graphs by Schenkerian scholars you study, the more you will encounter neat ways to convey musical features. In the end, it does not matter exactly which conventions you follow so long as what you do is clear and consistent.

Example 5.11 Bach, Chorale No. 320, from Felix Salzer's *Structural Hearing*
Source: Salzer 1982: Figure 327

Nevertheless, if you want your work to be read by others, it would be wise not to stray too far from the notational conventions outlined above.

Deciding how much detail to include is one of the hardest presentational issues. If a graph is too cluttered with foreground features, then it is hard for a reader to discern the overall shape; on the other hand, your analysis will not be convincing unless you clearly show how the deeper levels relate to the surface. Usually a mixture of graphs with different levels of detail is necessary if you want readers to grasp a complex analysis. It is all a waste of time, however, if it is not possible to relate graphs to the score, to each other and to your commentary, which means that you need to make lavish use of measure numbers. Readers will generally only be prepared to put in a certain amount of time and effort into understanding your work, so you should not erect unnecessary barriers. Music publishing packages such as

Example 5.12 Beethoven, Piano Sonata, Op. 109, third movement, Theme, from
Forte and Gilbert's *Introduction to Schenkerian Analysis*

Source: Forte and Gilbert 1982: Examples 272b and c. From *Introduction to Schenkerian Analysis*
by Allen Forte and Steven E. Gilbert. Copyright 1982 by W. W. Norton & Company. Used by
permission of W. W. Norton & Company.

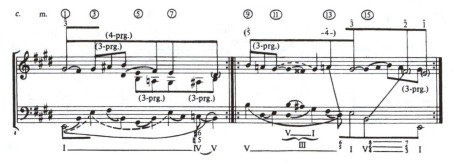

Sibelius and Finale allow clear graphs to be produced relatively easily. The
advantage of working in this way is that you can continually revise and
improve the detailed notation of your analysis in its final version. Tips on
producing Schenkerian graphs in various software packages can be found
on www.SchenkerGUIDE.com.

Part III

Analysis in practice

Chapter 6

Schenkerian analysis and form

Schenker's approach to form and structure is both bold and novel. Instead of breaking a piece down into static parts that make up a whole (first theme, second theme, codetta etc.), he describes music as a dynamic process of tonal tension and resolution. Schenker places the *Ursatz* with its tension-resolving journey from $\hat{3}$ or $\hat{5}$ down to $\hat{1}$ at the centre of this process. It is the way in which the progress of the *Urlinie* towards $\hat{1}$ is prolonged and delayed that creates the dynamic shape of the piece. However much the resolution of the *Urlinie* onto $\hat{1}$ is delayed, this tension is still underpinned by the fundamental unity of the *Ursatz* as the contrapuntal realization of the tonic. This is the essence of Schenker's understanding of form: a piece of tonal music is a unified elaboration of the tonic that defers structural closure in various ways in order to create its unique dramatic shape. It is with this conception of music as a dynamic unfolding that he revitalizes the traditional approach to large-scale structure.

Schenker's most basic formal distinction is between divided and undivided form. Undivided form is the result of an unbroken progression of the *Urlinie* that is understood as a single and continuous contrapuntal realization of the tonic, however long the piece (Example 6.1a). As discussed in Chapters 3 and 4, divided form is the result of interruption, in which the *Urlinie* descent is stopped and restarted. Two-part forms are most often the result of interruption (see Example 6.1b) while three-part forms spring from elaborations of interruptions or, for example, a neighbor note (Example 6.1c). The neighbor note, however, does not create an unequivocal structural division in the same way as the interruption; the neighbor note in Example 6.1c would only create a division if the piece was divided into clear sections in its final shape in the foreground, a classic example being a Minuet/Trio/Minuet structure.

Schenker therefore subsumes all formal divisions into the single sweep of the *Urlinie*. This approach to music is clearly aesthetic as much as technical; it involves making an active choice to interpret pieces as the unfolding and resolution of a single tension. Schenker's aesthetic of unity and dramatic tension seems particularly appropriate for music of Beethoven, but it is an

Example 6.1 Divided and undivided forms

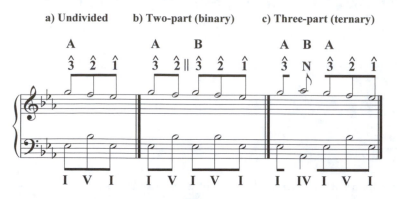

interesting question as to how well it serves the music of some other composers. In this chapter, I look first at a Beethoven movement in which Schenker's approach is very much at home and then at a Chopin piece for which it is a less immediately obvious fit. The remainder of the chapter is devoted to a discussion of one of the most important Classical large-scale structural paradigms, sonata form.

Allegretto from Beethoven's Piano Sonata, Op. 14, No. 1

The second movement of Beethoven's Piano Sonata in E major, Op. 14, No. 1 fits well with Schenker's idea of divided form. As outlined below, the E minor Allegretto section very tangibly draws out the tension of a descent from $\hat{3}$, displaying a clear two-part interrupted form (despite its slightly unusual lack of repeats). This is followed by a C major trio section, which eventually leads back to a repeat of the Allegretto. This is music with a clear sense of direction, a quality that Schenkerian analysis is particularly good at demonstrating. To get to grips with this movement you will need a copy of the music and either nimble enough fingers to play it through or a recording.

Example 6.2 shows how first the two phrases of the Allegretto outline a miniature interrupted *Urlinie* descent from $\hat{3}$ in m. 1 to $\hat{1}$ in m. 16 (shown by the caretted numbers in brackets). The details of this small-scale interruption mirror the phrase structure of the music: the end of the first eight-measure phrase is marked by the interruption, while the second reprises the same material but this time continuing the descent to $\hat{1}$. According to the principle of obligatory register outlined in Chapter 3, however, this descent cannot represent the final closure of the movement because of the register transfer of $\hat{3}$ up an octave in m. 9. The music from the opening is

Example 6.2 Beethoven, Piano Sonata in E major, Op. 14, No. 1, Allegretto, mm. 1–16

transposed up an octave so that the descending third arrives on $\hat{1}$ over the tonic in a different register from that established at the beginning. The perfect cadence in m. 15 therefore feels lacking, and the tensions of the piece will not be resolved until there has been a descent in the original register. Schenker's understanding of form relies on the idea that we expect particular types of closure. This will typically involve a descending linear motion to $\hat{1}$ over the tonic in the register established at the beginning of a piece. The extract in Example 6.2 does not fulfill that expectation and therefore creates a logic, or even a necessity, of continuation.

It is worth noting a couple of details from Example 6.2a before exploring the rest of the movement. I am concentrating initially on the tensional arch of the piece, asking how the music sets up the tension of $\hat{3}$ and then prolongs its resolution. The Allegretto starts with an unfolding from E to G that introduces the *Kopfton*; most of the first 16 measures can then be understood as a prolongation of this $\hat{3}$. In this movement, the tension of $\hat{3}$ is heightened in the foreground by the fact that the arrival on G in m. 3 is accompanied by a diminished seventh and a dramatic sforzando. The top line moves down from this high point of tension towards $\hat{1}$, but the temporary arrival on this goal at the beginning of m. 5 is undermined both because it is supported by a first inversion rather than a root position tonic and also because the melodic line regains G at the end of the measure. The prolongation of $\hat{3}$ therefore continues until m. 7, where a half close on the dominant underpins an elaboration of $\hat{2}$. The pattern is very much the same in the second phrase of the extract, except for the fact that $\hat{2}$ continues down to $\hat{1}$.

The defining feature of the first 16 measures, then, is the upwards register transfer in m. 9, which means that the overarching descent from $\hat{3}$ to $\hat{1}$ concludes an octave higher than it began. Example 6.3 shows what happens when this material is reprised in m. 33: the first phrase begins in the higher register before being subjected to a descending register transfer in m. 41 into the lower register for the second phrase, reversing the pattern from before. The music otherwise follows much the same course—an interrupted descent from $\hat{3}$ to $\hat{1}$—so the descent onto $\hat{1}$ in m. 51 now fulfills Schenker's criteria for satisfactory structural closure by being in the register established at the beginning. We can now see the basic dramatic shape of the piece: the initial 16 measures create a tension by shifting into a higher register, while the reprise resolves that tension by moving from the upper octave back into the original register. The resolution of this tension is slightly delayed, however, by a modification that Beethoven makes to the reprise of the second phrase. Measures 41–2 are the same as their equivalents at mm. 9–10, but in m. 43 the music leaps to C rather than the expected G, which results in the phrase being extended by three measures. As shown in the analysis, the C turns out to be the beginning of a third progression that leads onto an extended elaboration of A. This A is ultimately a neighbor note onto the G at m. 49, which is the note that was originally expected

Example 6.3 Beethoven, Piano Sonata in E major, Op. 14, No. 1, Allegretto, mm. 33–51

in m. 43. The previous six measures can therefore be understood as a delaying of resolution—the neighbor note introduces a new harmonic and linear tension that ultimately heightens the effect of the closure when it occurs in m. 51.

Example 6.4 puts the first sixteen-measure phrase (A) and its modified reprise at m. 33 (A') in their wider context—the pattern of two small-scale interruption structures with symmetrically balancing register transfers can clearly be seen. As shown in Example 6.4, my suggestion is that these two local interrupted *Urlinien* are part of a larger interrupted descent from $\hat{3}$ across the whole piece. The *Urlinie* descent across the first sixteen measures is shown as a prolongation of $\hat{3}$, which moves to $\hat{2}$ only in m. 32. This overall structure again involves a register transfer, with the point of interruption displaced up an octave. The main body of the descent, however, in line with Schenker's ideas on structural register, all takes place within the same octave (i.e. the $\hat{3}$ at the beginning and the $\hat{2}$–$\hat{1}$ at mm. 50–1). The difference between a register transfer and a coupling was discussed in Chapter 3: the former displaces notes of the *Urlinie* while the latter creates long-term structural connections between two registers. This Allegretto shifts the middle of its interruption structure up an octave and this part of the *Urlinie* does not appear in the main register. As a result, this is probably best understood as a register transfer as it constitutes a displacement of rather than a connection between registers.

The only part of this larger-scale interruption structure that we have not already seen is the B section from m. 17, an extract from which is shown in Example 6.5. These eight measures lead back into the reprise at m. 33. The reprise is prepared for by a pause on the dominant at m. 32, which represents the main interruption of the *Urlinie* shown on Example 6.4. Despite Schenker's rethinking of form, it is actually typical for the structural division of the *Urlinie* to coincide with the traditional formal division of the movement in this way. If the first 16 measures can be understood as a prolongation of $\hat{3}$ through a local descent in E minor, mm. 25–29 elaborate the same scale

Example 6.4 Beethoven, Piano Sonata in E major, Op. 14, No. 1, Allegretto, mm. 1–62, middleground analysis

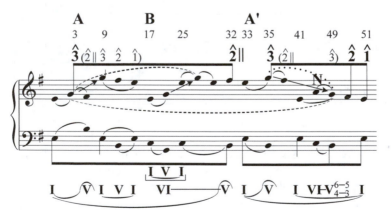

degree in a different way. These few measures are spanned by a decorated consonant skip from G to E, but the harmonic context is now completely different—not E minor but C major (chord VI in relation to the tonic). From a Schenkerian point of view, this constitutes a further delaying of the inevitable final closure onto $\hat{1}$ and thus a continuation of the structural tension of $\hat{3}$. Measures 17–24 (shown only in outline on Example 6.4) follow a similar pattern to Example 6.5: it starts with the same passage an octave lower before ending on the dominant of C.

A traditional formal analysis would show the various sections of this piece along with their motivic and harmonic content. A Schenkerian view, however, is more dynamic, interpreting music in terms of a single motion towards a goal (closure on $\hat{1}$) that is beset by "obstacles, reverses . . . detours, expansions, interpolations, and, in short, retardations of all kinds."[1] The first "retardation" shown in Example 6.4 is the transfer of register at m. 9, the second is the detour to chord VI at m. 17, and so the piece unfolds until closure is achieved in m. 51. This is not, however, the end of the Allegretto. As discussed previously, the arrival on $\hat{1}$, which is the structural end of a piece, does not necessarily have to be the actual end. Although

Example 6.5 Beethoven, Piano Sonata in E major, Op. 14, No. 1, Allegretto, mm. 25–32

locating the final descent onto $\hat{1}$ is not always straightforward, there is nothing particularly mysterious about this process either—the *Urlinie* final descent is essentially the last plausible $\hat{2}$ to $\hat{1}$ motion that occurs over a V–I in the obligatory register.

This is essentially how Schenker redefines the traditional notion of a coda, which he describes as any music that occurs after the final arrival on $\hat{1}$.[2] Example 6.6 shows the coda of this Allegretto, and again Schenkerian and traditional notions of form coincide. A traditional formal analysis would designate this passage as a coda for several reasons: first, it represents an "extra" phrase in relation to the first appearance of the A section; second, it largely consists of a series of cadential gestures; third, it employs a thematic device sometimes called liquidation—the repetition of a small thematic fragment (the eighth-note figure originally heard in m. 4). From a Schenkerian point of view, there is no further hint of a descent in the main register— the passage consists instead of a series of neighbor notes that prolong $\hat{1}$ in various octaves.

Although the Allegretto is therefore basically a two-part structure, divided around the point of interruption in m. 32, it is part of what traditional theory would designate as larger ternary form. A Maggiore section immediately follows the Allegretto after which the whole movement is rounded off with a da capo. Many minuet and trio forms of this type consist of two more-or-less independent movements, but a Schenkerian analysis will generally attempt to show how the whole structure is unified. For minor key minuets that follow the common pattern of moving to the tonic major for the trio, this sense of unity is often little more than conceptual. As shown in Example 6.7, in such cases the minuet and trio each have an independent *Ursatz* structure, but the whole can be understood as a prolongation of the minuet's *Ursatz* by means of "mixture" (i.e. the change from minor to major).

Beethoven's Maggiore trio in Op. 14, No. 1, however, can be understood as part of a unified movement in a more fundamental sense. Most of the Maggiore consists of varied repetitions of and developments on the C major

Example 6.6 Beethoven, Sonata in E major, Op. 14, No. 1, Allegretto, mm. 51–61

Example 6.7 Typical structure for minuet and trio

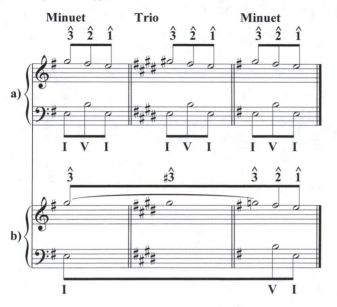

passage from mm. 89–95 (shown in Example 6.8). The trio is therefore, from a Schenkerian perspective, a tonicization of chord VI. As such the whole Maggiore section can be understood as a hugely extended neighbor note (C) in the bass to the home dominant (B) and therefore is not a self-contained structure like that of the trio in Example 6.7. There is also another sense in which this structure unifies the movement as a whole: the structural basis for the B section of the Allegretto is also a prolongation of chord VI as neighbor note to the dominant (see Example 6.5). The way in which the same elaboration is extended in the trio can therefore be understood as an organic development of an earlier idea, helping further to unify the two sections of the second movement.

Chopin, Grande Valse Brilliante, Op. 18

The second movement of Beethoven's E major piano sonata is interpreted in the above analysis as a continuous and dynamic unfolding. Schenker's *Ursatz* is most at home in pieces such as this in which there is a genuine feeling of unbroken momentum from beginning to end. The only point before m. 51 where there is any real possibility of closure is m. 16, and even without Schenker's concept of obligatory register it is clear that this cannot be the end of the movement. Similarly, the suggestion that the middle section of this ternary structure is subsumed into the overall sense of forward momentum only expresses something that is already intuitively felt. Not all

Example 6.8 Beethoven, Piano Sonata in E major, Op. 14, No. 1, Allegretto, end of Maggiore into recapitulation of Allegretto

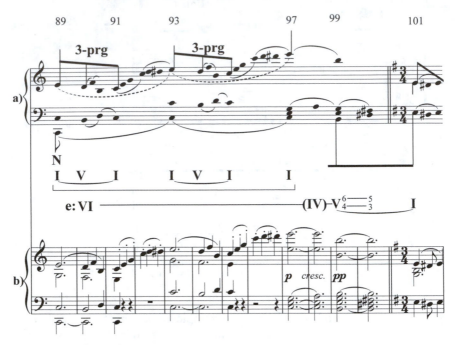

pieces, however, correspond to the aesthetic of *Ursatz* quite so readily. Chopin's Op. 18 *Grande Valse Brilliante* in E♭ major is, like many such works, made up of a number of fairly short and contrasting sections that are variously repeated and developed. This structure does not fit quite so happily with Schenker's notion of a continuous unfolding from beginning to end and, while this does not mean that there is no point analyzing such a piece, we have to take a slightly different approach. Although you will be able to grasp the gist of the following analysis just from the examples given, you will again need to consult the score if you really want to see how the piece is put together.

Once the waltz has established its rhythmic momentum at m. 5, the shape of the opening paragraph (shown in Example 6.9) is quite clear: the top line builds towards the sforzando B♭ in m. 8, from which there is a descending line from $\hat{5}$ to $\hat{1}$. Unlike the beginning of the Beethoven, which moved away from the opening register, this does not pose any particular structural problem. Leaving aside the obvious point that the piece would be absurdly short if it ended here, there is no structural reason why it should not do so: the twelve measures outline an ascent to a *Kopfton* ($\hat{5}$) from which there is a descent to $\hat{1}$ over a perfect cadence in the tonic.

Example 6.9 Chopin, *Grande Valse Brilliante*, Op. 18, mm. 1–12

Many of Chopin's shorter pieces, in fact, both start and end with the same structurally closed paragraph. In such cases the earlier descents are treated as decorations of their *Kopftonen*, while the last repeat of the material forms the structural *Urlinie* descent—this is also the analytical strategy taken in the minuet structure outlined in Example 6.7. The idea of a movement as a single motion from beginning to end is obviously not so strong in such pieces, because there are many points at which they could theoretically come to a satisfactory close. This should not be seen as a problem. It is simply that the dramatic structure (and indeed the aesthetic) of a movement that consists of repeated structurally closed sections is obviously rather different from one that unfolds organically from beginning to end. Although Chopin's Op. 18 waltz is a comparatively lengthy work, and quite a bit more structurally complicated than some of his shorter pieces, the *Ursatz* does not necessarily span the whole movement in the easily traceable way suggested in the analysis of the Beethoven Allegretto above.

After the extract shown in Example 6.9, there is a nearly exact repeat of mm. 5–12, after which this whole section is repeated again. The first paragraph of this waltz, in other words, entails four descents from $\hat{5}$ to $\hat{1}$ in Eb, played back to back. I would suggest that Chopin achieves two things with this relentless repetition: first, he very strongly establishes the key in a piece that will modulate extensively as it develops; second, he creates a very strong impression of this opening tune in our minds, so that when he abandons this material for over 100 measures in the middle of the waltz we nevertheless strongly anticipate its return, making its eventual reprise more satisfying.

The first new material appears in m. 20, as shown in Example 6.10. As can be seen from the analysis, this is essentially a rhapsody on the $\hat{1}$ reached at the end of the previous section. This Eb is decorated by a series of neighbor notes and is given a new harmonic context in m. 21 as $\hat{5}$ in Ab (IV in relation to the tonic). Unlike the previous section, this does not have the same strong sense of closure, with the Eb unfolding up to a G before resolving onto to a weakly projected $\hat{1}$ in Ab over a perfect cadence. This material is

Example 6.10 Chopin, *Grande Valse Brilliante*, Op. 18, mm. 20–8

again repeated, the only real difference being that the final measure is a half-note A♭, thus creating a slightly less fleeting sense of closure.

This leads back into a written-out repeat of pretty much everything heard so far, starting at m. 27 and ending in m. 68. The music then moves on to introduce several new ideas, first in D♭ major and eventually in G♭. I do not propose to look at this central section of the piece here, but instead I move straight to the reprise of the opening material, which takes place at m. 189. The material is recapitulated almost unchanged until a final repeat of the emphatic ascent to 5̂ first seen in m. 5. Instead of continuing as before from 5̂ in m. 232 (not shown) there are nearly three measures of rests followed by the passage shown in Example 6.11. Chopin can now reap the rewards of his relentless repetition of this opening material, in that he is able to play on our expectations. He stops again when the descending line reaches 2̂ in m. 237. One possible analysis of this waltz is that this 2̂ is the part of the final *Urlinie* descent—if so, the rest of the piece from mm. 240 onwards is an extended coda. The final section continues in much the same vein as mm. 239–47 in Example 6.11, so this analysis makes sense in that the music seems to act as an extended emphasis of the tonic. As can be seen on the example, however, one of the ways in which Chopin extends this coda section is by picking up on a harmonic implication that goes right back to m. 8. The tonic chord in m. 8 includes a flattened seventh and thus sounds briefly as if it might take us towards the subdominant—an implication that the coda exploits in full.

Haydn, Divertimento in C major, Hob. XVI, No. 10

The symphonies and sonatas of Mozart, Haydn and Beethoven lie right at the heart of Schenker's area of interest, so it is inevitable that he addresses the question of sonata form. He characteristically proclaims that "it is necessary to discard the concepts and terminology of conventional theory," proposing instead an understanding of sonata form based on the *Ursatz*.[3] Analysts in Schenker's day had a tendency to discuss sonata form almost exclusively in terms of themes, which in his view showed an undue concern for the surface at the expense of the deeper structure. The influential pianist and writer Charles Rosen also considers a solely thematic approach inadequate, pointing out, among other things, that Haydn frequently wrote sonata form movements using just one theme.[4] Rosen suggests that the basic principle behind sonata form is something much more fundamental than a series of contrasting themes: "sonata forms open with a clearly defined opposition . . . which is intensified and then symmetrically resolved."[5] This opposition is not, however, primarily a thematic one, but rather one between tonic (first subject) and either dominant or relative major (second subject). The intensification of this harmonic tension occurs in the development (usually by means of various modulations), culminating in a return to the dominant

Example 6.11 Chopin, *Grande Valse Brilliante*, Op. 18, mm. 234–47

by the end of this section. Finally, symmetrical resolution is achieved in the recapitulation by the transposition of the second subject material into the tonic. For both Rosen and Schenker, the thematic presentation of this scheme is secondary to the harmonic tension and resolution. Rosen, for example, extends the "sonata principle" to movements other than the classic first movement "sonata allegro"; in slow movements, the development can be omitted without doing any violence to the basic idea of tonic/dominant opposition followed by resolution.

Schenker likewise pares down the concept of sonata form, concentrating solely on linear-harmonic structure; he suggests that the interrupted *Ursatz* is particularly associated with sonata form.[6] As shown in the descent from $\hat{3}$ in Example 6.12a (the simplest of the interrupted structures), Schenker's conception of sonata form relates interestingly to Rosen's: first, the clearly defined opposition of tonic and dominant is expressed as one between the prolongation of $\hat{3}$ and that of $\hat{2}$; second, the development continues the elaboration of the dominant (corresponding to Rosen's intensification); finally, the recapitulation achieves the resolution of a single descent to $\hat{1}$ into which the previous dominant elaborations associated with the second subject are integrated. As so often with Schenker, what is really interesting about his description of sonata form is the way in which it complements rather than obliterates ideas from traditional formal analysis. The three models outlined in Example 6.12 all have the same basic dramatic arch: a tension is introduced by the tonicization of either III or V at the end of the exposition, which continued through the development, and resolved in the recapitulation. The first two models are those most often found in Schenker's own analyses, while the third is a variant proposed by Ernst Oster, the translator and editor of *Free Composition*.

The majority of examples in this book have been chosen because a Schenkerian analysis has a distinctive contribution to make to the interpretation of the piece, or, at least, that the analysis presents certain features particularly clearly. The Haydn sonata movement analyzed below, however, has been chosen because it exemplifies some of the practical and theoretical problems as well as the advantages of a Schenkerian approach.

The exposition of Haydn's Divertimento in C major (Example 6.13) demonstrates the potential danger of focusing too narrowly on the technique in sonata form analysis of identifying first subject, transition and second subject. The first three phrases (beginning at mm. 1, 9 and 13) are, from a motivic point of view, developments of the same basic idea as shown in Example 6.13b. Each time a variation of motif X is followed by a passage starting with motif Y—this is perhaps least clear in the second phrase, where the first two semiquavers of the Y motif are inverted. By the time the third phrase has ended at the beginning of m. 16, the dominant (G major) has already been firmly established; this creates a slight problem for any analyst determined to find clearly defined divisions into themes or subject groups. The traditional solution would be to suggest that these first three phrases are respectively first subject (m. 1), transition (m. 5) and second subject (m. 9); sonata form movements in which the same motivic material is used in both first and second subject groups in this way are sometimes referred to as monothematic. According to this analysis, the passage that begins in the second half of m. 16 would be understood as the beginning of a closing subject—it introduces new thematic material after a clear cadence in the dominant. The only other possible solution, that of designating m.

Example 6.12 Sonata forms: (a) Descent from $\hat{3}$; (b) Descent from $\hat{5}$ in the minor; (c) Descent from $\hat{5}$ with inner voice $\hat{3}$

Sources:
(a) Extrapolated from Schenker 1977: Figure 47/1
(b) Extrapolated from Schenker 1977: Figure 154/3
(c) Extrapolated from Oster's extended footnote in Schenker 1977: 139–40

a)

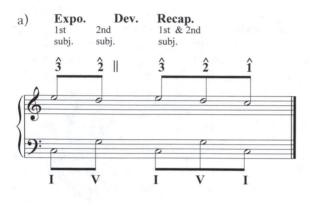

b)

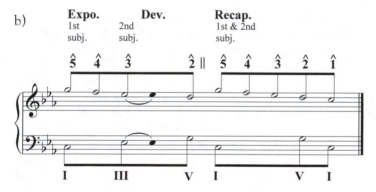

c)

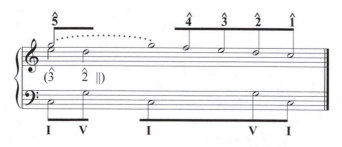

16 onwards as the beginning of the second subject, would be odd, not least because it feels like a continuation and conclusion of the preceding material. The above analysis shows how the exposition is developed out of the initial four-measure phrase; where it is less successful is in explaining the overall shape of the exposition and the relationship of this shape to general principles that would apply to any sonata form movement.

A Schenkerian approach to this exposition also has its strengths and weaknesses. Whereas the first eight measures present some problems that are discussed below, the analysis on the lower staves of Example 6.13 is most successful in its interpretation of the passage from m. 9 to the end of the extract. I suggested above that this music might be divided into second subject and closing subject; a Schenkerian analysis, however, opens up the possibility of understanding it as a single arch.

It would be a tediously long-winded exercise to describe in prose every elaboration in this passage; part of the point of a Schenkerian graph is that there should be no need to do so. I will therefore outline only the overall shape of the phrase, leaving you to spend some time looking at the finer details. Measures 9–12 can be understood as an arpeggiation from G to D. Although this arpeggiation involves ascending motion, there is a descending register transfer from the higher B in m. 9 to the lower B in m. 12, so that it ends at a lower pitch than its starting point (that this is the right interpretation is confirmed in the recapitulation of the same material, in which this register transfer does not take place). Measures 13–21 constitute a descending fifth progression from the same D down to the G at the end of the extract. Measures 13–15 can be understood as an elaboration of D, after which the beginning of the closing subject at the end of m. 16 moves us down through a dominant seventh (C) to an elaboration of B, which descends to G at the final cadence. From a Schenkerian perspective, the closing theme is not a separate entity at all, because it begins part of the way through a descending fifth progression. In fact, the whole passage from m. 9 to the end can be understood as a self-contained elaboration of the dominant, with an arpeggiation across mm. 9–12 followed by a descending fifth progression that prolongs $\hat{2}$ over V. Similarly, the first eight measures, to which I shall return later, can be understood as a prolongation of an underlying progression from $\hat{3}$ to $\hat{2}$, corresponding to the move from tonic to dominant across the first subject and transition that I suggested in the traditional formal analysis. One advantage of a Schenkerian approach is that it shows clearly how the opposition of tonic and dominant is articulated in this passage. The first eight measures move onto the dominant (ending on an imperfect cadence), after which the rest of the exposition consists of a tonicization of this dominant in the form of a prolongation of $\hat{2}$.

Rosen's model of opposition/intensification/resolution reduces sonata form to its absolute essentials. Instead of trying to fit a piece of music into the rigid (and somewhat dubious) framework of traditional formal models, one

Example 6.13 Haydn, Divertimento in C major, Hob. XVI, No. 10, Moderato, mm. 1–23

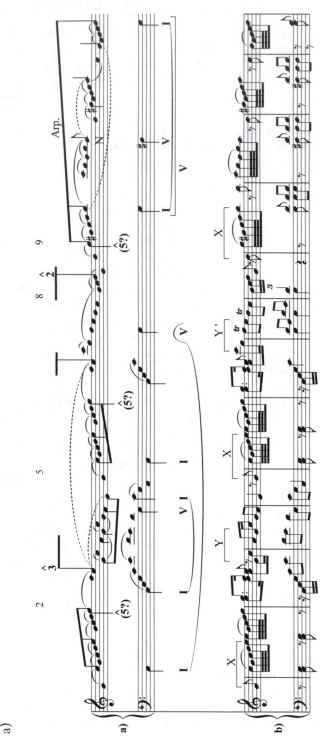

asks the more useful question of how the opposition of dominant and tonic is articulated in terms of a wide range of parameters, usually including motivic content. The beauty of Rosen's framework, in other words, lies in its simplicity and flexibility. As we have seen, Schenker's sonata form model is based on a somewhat similar idea; the difference is that the harmonic opposition and resolution is expressed in terms of a linear-harmonic framework.

In working out the details of how this movement introduces and resolves its oppositions, we are presented with a practical problem of whether the *Kopfton* (the initial note of the *Urlinie*) is $\hat{3}$ or $\hat{5}$. The problem is that while G seems to be quite prominent at the beginning of the piece (see those notes marked $\hat{5}$? between the staffs on Example 6.13a), it is very difficult to find an analysis in terms of a descending *Urlinie* from this scale degree. As discussed in Chapter 3, a descent from $\hat{5}$ needs a harmonically supported $\hat{4}$ (in this case F). The only real candidates are in mm. 2 and 6, and, in both cases, the F is dissonant against a C major harmony. It is too late by m. 9 because the music has moved into G major by this point, thus replacing F naturals with F sharps. If the Gs are too prominent to ignore and if it is also possible to find a convincing descent from $\hat{5}$ in the recapitulation, one solution would be the model suggested in Example 6.12c. The descent already marked from $\hat{3}$ to $\hat{2}$ in Example 6.13 would then be considered as a lower voice in the context of an overarching prolongation of $\hat{5}$.

Schenker does not offer much in the way of particular models for the development, and as this section of the Moderato from Hob. XVI: 10 is relatively straightforward, it is only in the recapitulation of the material from the exposition (shown in Example 6.14) that we again encounter issues relevant to sonata form analysis in general.

One initial question to ask of a recapitulation is how the exposition material is re-composed so that it remains in the tonic, instead of modulating to the dominant.[7] Haydn keeps things fairly simple in the recapitulation of the Moderato, with changes kept to a minimum. As at the beginning, the first eight measures of Example 6.14 close on the dominant, and are left unchanged save for a few small details. The rest of passage is also pretty much the same, except for the obvious and crucial difference that the passage from m. 55 (the equivalent of m. 9) is in the tonic rather than the dominant. The only other significant change is that the register transfers around m. 12 and its equivalent point at m. 58 are handled slightly differently.

In terms of Rosen's description of sonata form, the recapitulation is the point at which the opposition between tonic and dominant is resolved. From a Schenkerian perspective, this same problem is expressed in slightly different terms, asking how the recapitulation becomes part of the overarching *Ursatz* prolongation. Its task is therefore to integrate the elaborations of tonic ($\hat{3}$) and dominant ($\hat{2}$) from the exposition into a unified descent. The main obstacle to this is the transposition of the elaboration of $\hat{2}$ into the tonic. What was a descending fifth progression from $\hat{2}$ in mm. 9–21 (Example 6.13)

Example 6.14 Haydn, Divertimento in C major, Hob. XVI, No. 10, Moderato, mm. 47–68

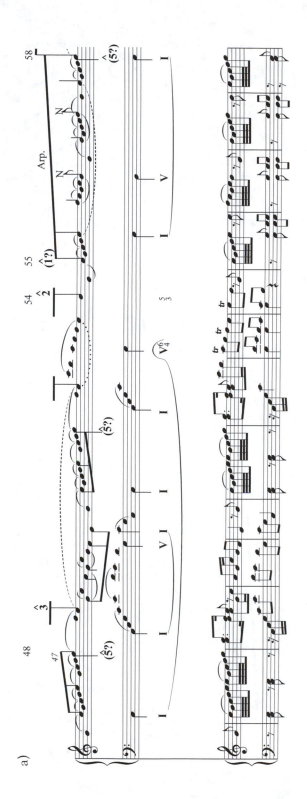

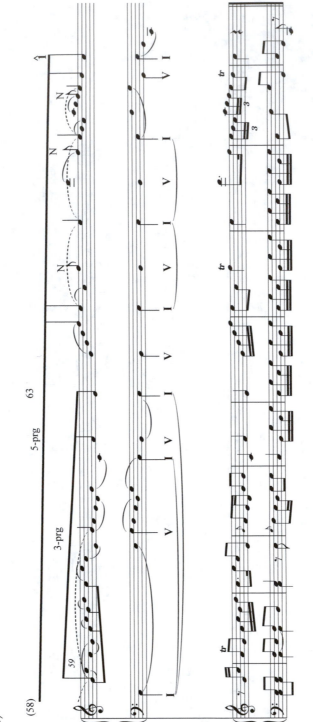

becomes a descent from $\hat{5}$ to $\hat{1}$ (mm. 58–67 in Example 6.14). This can be seen more clearly in Example 6.15, which is a middleground summary, with measure numbers that correspond to Examples 6.13 and 6.14.

When $\hat{2}$ is prolonged by a descending fifth progression in the context of an *Urlinie* descent from $\hat{3}$, as in this example, it poses a particular (and very common) challenge: subsuming the fifth progression into the overall descent of the *Urlinie* to $\hat{1}$. In *Free Composition*, both Schenker and Ernst Oster (the translator/editor) suggest various ways in which a recapitulation might integrate the second subject's descending fifth, but Example 6.15 is the only solution specifically mentioned in Schenker's discussion of sonata form. He writes that "a fifth progression is frequently superimposed on the final third progression. There is no doubt that the primary tone remains the $\hat{3}$; the fifth-progression is merely a final reinforcement."[8]

The sense of a final reinforcement can be seen very clearly on Example 6.15. In the exposition, the descending fifth progression at m. 12 only serves to prolong the $\hat{2}$ that has already been stated at m. 8. When this material returns in the recapitulation it now performs the same function in relation to $\hat{1}$. The arrival on $\hat{1}$ is therefore at m. 55; although stopping at this point would make for rather an abrupt ending, the large-scale closure of the descent has nevertheless been achieved.

In this model, the dominant material from the beginning is subsumed into the large-scale linear harmonic structure by being relegated to the status of a sort of extended coda. In some respects, this is a tempting interpretation for this particular piece; the sense of the main business being over at the beginning of m. 55 is partly why I find the recapitulation of this work slightly unsatisfactory. On the other hand, we have come to this reading by ignoring the prominent $\hat{5}$ that recurs throughout exposition and recapitulation, an oversight that should perhaps be addressed.

Example 6.15 Haydn, Divertimento in C major, Hob. XVI, No. 10, Moderato, analysis as descent from $\hat{3}$

Source: After model as suggested in Schenker 1977: Figure 35/1

Example 6.16 offers an alternative interpretation, based on the model proposed by Oster and outlined in Example 6.12c above, which takes the 5̂ at the beginning much more seriously. In this reading, the exposition unfolds a third from 5̂, introducing 3̂ as an inner voice, This inner voice then moves down to D at m. 8, before another unfolding takes the melody back to the upper voice G at m. 9. From here, the register transfer in the middle of the arpeggiation that begins in m. 9 means that the fifth progression elaborates D in m. 12 back in the lower register. In terms of the *Ursatz*, 5̂ is therefore the principal voice in the exposition, from which there is no descent.

The transposition of the dominant material in the recapitulation has a dramatic effect. After the initial unfolding of 5̂ to 3̂ from m. 47 and the stepwise move down to D in m. 54, the transposition means that the arpeggiation at m. 55 now unfolds from C back up to 5̂. From here, the fifth progression originally heard at m. 12 becomes the main structural descent to 1̂, casting it in a very different light to the previous interpretation. Instead of being extra concluding material after the main structural close, this descending fifth progression becomes the crucial *Urlinie* descent that resolves the linear contrapuntal tensions of the whole movement.

There is a legitimate debate to be had as to what extent the integration of the fifth progression into an overall descent from 3̂ in sonata form movements is a genuinely musical problem or arises from the difficulties of reconciling complex music to a simple background structure. Either way, I have tried to demonstrate in this chapter that graphs of background structure offer an elegant way of articulating the dynamics of the major Classical forms.

Example 6.16 Haydn, Divertimento in C major, Hob. XVI, No. 10, Moderato, analysis as descent from 5̂

Source: After model implicitly suggested by Ernst Oster in Schenker 1977: 139

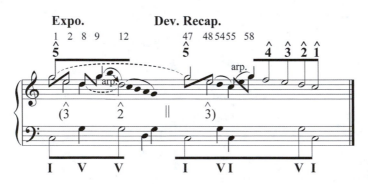

The interruption structure provides a basic model for the dramatic tension of the binary forms of Beethoven and others, while in ternary forms (e.g. the Minuet and Trio or the Chopin Grand Valse) a Schenkerian graph can expose a basic unity of structure that is not immediately obvious. Finally, the opposition of tonic and dominant areas in a sonata form exposition and their eventual synthesis in the recapitulation can be graphed in a way that is both economical and sophisticated.

Chapter 7

Playing with register

The most interesting and convincing analytical work addresses a clearly defined question or issue. It may do so explicitly, as in Schenker's short polemic "Abolish the phrasing slur"[1] or implicitly as in the case of his *Five Graphic Analyses* (Schenker 1969), which are offered without any commentary. Whether an analysis is presented as prose or in diagrammatic form, it is ultimately a technical description of the music; it is only when this is evaluated and interpreted that it becomes really interesting.

One of the central concerns of Schenker's mature work is showing how the surface of the music is the result of a series of transformations from the background. He believes that this allows us to understand "the long-range vision of our great composers."[2] Because Schenker is convinced that only the real masters of tonal composition are capable of creating such large-scale connections, the idea of the artist as genius becomes crucial for his theories. According to Schenker, the "power of will and imagination which lives through the transformations of a masterwork [from background to foreground] reaches us in our spirit as the power of imagination . . . the life of the transformations conveys its own nature to us."[3] Although Schenker is careful to make a case here for the relevance of his proposed structures whether or not they are ordinarily perceived, he ultimately believes that it is only through these techniques that we can get anywhere near understanding a composer's genius.[4] We may be uncomfortable with such ideas and with Schenker's restrictive definition of musical culture based on the work of a handful of German composers, but a less extreme form of these views was and is still quite widespread.[5] Although most writers now shy away from such terms as masterwork and genius, much analytical work is still informed by the dominant idea in twentieth-century music theory that a musical work forms a coherent whole and that it unfolds organically (or at least logically) from its beginning to its end.

A common way of addressing this issue is to ask how a piece of music is derived from its basic materials, a question that traditional analysis often addresses in terms of motives and themes. The analyst will identify motivic material at the beginning of a piece before exploring how this material is repeated and varied. This is traditionally complemented with an overview of the piece's tonal structure and an analysis of any unusual or interesting harmonic devices. Such an approach seeks to find an internal logic that might either reflect the creative processes of the composer or affect the way in which we hear the piece. This logic may be internal to the music, or the analyst may choose to understand the musical events dramatically. If a piece, for example, begins with two highly contrasting themes that are later reconciled, this can be understood as a purely musical process or it can be described as if the themes were players in some sort of drama. An analyst might write of contrasting musical material battling it out in the development of a sonata form movement, for example, or the work as a whole might describe a journey from tragedy to triumph.

In describing the formal and dramatic structure of musical works, Schenker employs a range of extravagant biological and psychological metaphors, in *Free Composition* comparing music both to life and to speech:

> In the art of music, as in life, motion towards the goal encounters obstacles, reversals, disappointments, and involves great distances, detours, expansion, interpolations, and, in short, retardations of all kinds. Therein lies the source of all artistic delaying, from which the creative mind can derive content that is ever new. Thus we hear in the middle-ground and foreground an almost dramatic course of events.[6]
>
> [music] may simulate expectation, preparation, surprise, disappointment, patience, impatience and humor . . . music is never comparable to mathematics or to architecture, but only to language, a kind of tonal language.[7]

In *Der Tonwille* Schenker is even more explicitly anthropomorphic (i.e. attributing human characteristics to the music); he describes a motive as "a creature of flesh and blood that came into being in the deeper recesses of the master's tonal imagination."[8] Thus Schenker's writings positively encourage us to interpret musical structures dramatically, a point that needs making because this more fantastical side of his thought was less fashionable in the 1960s and 1970s—a fact reflected in writings from this period.

In this chapter I therefore follow two lines of analytical enquiry: first, an exploration of the processes by which a particular piece of music can be understood to develop its basic materials; second, how these processes can be interpreted in terms of a dramatic strategy. I am going to focus my enquiry, however, on the role of changes in register. The repetition of a melody up or down an octave is the simplest example of a change in register, but a slightly broader definition might also include the skips between voices that were discussed under the heading of unfolding in Chapters 2 and 3.

Changes in register can, however, be much more ostentatious, as in the short extract from Handel's *Messiah* in Example 7.1. Schenker would call

Example 7.1 Handel, *The Messiah*, "Thy rebuke hath broken his heart"

the compositional device used here a register transfer. The melody can be understood as a transformation of the much more ordinary neighbor-note figure shown in the second half of the example; by transferring this neighbor note down an octave and making the leap by means of two tritones, Handel creates a figure that graphically conveys the anguish of the text.

As we have already seen, this sort of register transfer, in which a melodic idea is split across different octaves, can occur in the background as well as on the surface of the music. If a note of the *Urlinie* is transferred up or down an octave, according to the principle of "obligatory register," it creates a structural tension that is usually resolved by the end of the movement, as seen in the previous chapter. In this chapter, I briefly explore two quite different dramatic uses of register transfer by Mozart and Beethoven; Mozart's is more immediately obvious, but Beethoven's has more far-reaching consequences.

Menuetto from Mozart's "Dissonance" Quartet

Example 7.2b shows the final section of the Menuetto from Mozart's "Dissonance" quartet in short score. In terms of traditional formal analysis, the whole movement is in rounded binary form, in which the B section is rounded off by a modified repeat of the A section—AB(A'), as shown in Example 7.2a. If the A section ends in the dominant (as is the case in this movement) it has to be re-written for the reprise so that it finishes in the tonic; it is this final modified A' section of the Menuetto that is reproduced in Example 7.2b.

As shown in Example 7.2a, the A' section descends from $\hat{3}$ to $\hat{1}$ as the concluding part of an interruption structure. The first half of the Menuetto (of which Example 7.2b is a modification) consists of an interrupted descent from $\hat{3}$–$\hat{2}$, while the beginning of the B section from mm. 21–40 elaborates a circle-of-fifths motion to the dominant in preparation for the return of the tonic in m. 40 (also not shown in the main part of Example 7.2). There is nothing unusual about this structure—rounded binary form movements usually outline this sort of interrupted descent from $\hat{3}$ or $\hat{5}$ —it is the way in which register is used in the final section (and indeed in the whole movement) that interests me.

The first phrase of Example 7.2b ends in m. 43 with the first violin leaping down an octave onto a dominant seventh. The sudden and rather disruptive lurch of this descending register transfer is heightened by the following quarter-note rest and by the fact that the seventh (F) is left unresolved. The octave unison eighth-note figure that follows also comes to a halt on F, and it is not until the same figure is repeated up an octave in m. 46 that the dominant seventh is decisively resolved in this new register (to E at the end of m. 47). As the analysis suggests, from a middleground perspective the eight-measure phrase (mm. 40–7) is simply an upper neighbor note prolongation of E; the change of register, however, helps to create a little local dramatic tension. The surface of the music, with its disjunctions of register, is unified by its relationship to the underlying neighbor note progression, but it is precisely this registral play on the surface of the music that brings the middleground neighbor note to life. The effectiveness of the descending register transfer (shown by a dotted slur) can be demonstrated by imagining how much less lively and interesting the passage would be if the first violin either introduced and resolved the dominant seventh straight away (as shown on Example 7.2c) or if mm. 43–5 were rewritten up an octave. A Schenkerian approach allows us to uncover a middleground simplicity that casts the complexities of the foreground in a new light; by constructing a "normalized" version of the voice-leading, we can see exactly what is distinctive about the passage in hand.

If the first eight measures of Example 7.2b are characterized by changes in register, in the next four measures the registral displacements are even more extreme. As shown in Example 7.3, the passage from the last beat of m. 47 to the last beat of m. 50 is basically an elaboration of a descending third progression from E—the small stave at the top of Example 7.3 shows

Example 7.2 Mozart, String Quartet in C major, K. 465, Menuetto: (a) Middleground summary; (b) Mm. 40–55; (c) Mm. 41–4 (re-written)

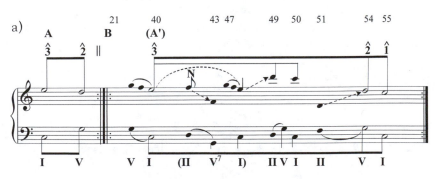

b)

I   II ——————V⁷

I   V⁷   I   IV   II — V   I

II ——————————————— V⁶₄   ⁵₃   I

c)

Notice in Example 7.2a how the Schenkerian graph shows the middleground of the passage in question in the context of the background for the whole movement. This sort of middleground summary, with its varying degrees of detail, is a very common and economical way of illustrating a particular analytical point, as discussed in Chapter 5.

Example 7.3 Mozart, String Quartet in C major, K. 465, Menuetto, mm. 48–51

the underlying voice-leading pattern in which E ($\hat{3}$) at the end of m. 47 is first decorated by a neighbor note F at the end of m. 48, followed by a descent through $\hat{2}$ to $\hat{1}$ on the last beats of the next two measures. Note how caretted numbers in brackets can be used to show descending lines that are not necessarily part of the main *Urlinie* descent.

It is in the first violin part that the most noticeable registral play occurs: the "normalized" third progression shown in the top staff is transformed by an upwards register transfer in m. 49, which results in the first violin arriving on a high D and then continuing the third progression in this register. This upwards displacement of the $\hat{2}$ and the $\hat{1}$ in mm. 49 and 50 makes the subsequent plunge down to the low D in m. 51 even more dramatic.

Before putting this series of register transfers in its context it is worth looking briefly at how the other voices in the top staff of Example 7.3 are distributed across the quartet texture. The most important connecting thread is the series of descending third progressions highlighted with diagonal lines on the top staff and with stems and beams on the score in Example 7.3. This eighth-note figure, which is decorated by unfolding the thirds in the top stave into constant skips, is passed downwards through the quartet from its initial appearance in the second violin in m. 48. When the cello takes up this idea it takes it down an octave, but here the register transfer is not made for dramatic purposes but in order to open out the instrumental texture. Notice too how the first violin begins each measure by reinforcing the first note of the accompanying third progression; the resulting consonant skips of a third both clarify the series of secondary dominant harmonies (i.e. V of IV etc.) and continue on a foreground level the interplay of registers that is so important to this movement.

The elaboration of the overarching descent from $\hat{3}$ over mm. 40–55 thus involves opening out the melodic line into three registers. The descent starts on E and, as Schenker's theory of the obligatory register predicts, the descent is finally completed in the same register in m. 55. The descending register transfer at m. 43 opens up a new lower register to which we return at the most dramatic leap of the passage in m. 51. This lower D is transferred back up to the obligatory register by means of two measures of ascending stepwise eighth notes in the first violin. As noted above, the arrival on D in m. 51 is preceded by the opening up of a new higher register in mm. 49 and 50. Unlike the lower register, there is the semblance of a descent through $\hat{2}$ to $\hat{1}$, although it is metrically weak and lacking in a strong supporting root progression into the cadence.

Although Schenker's principle of the obligatory register is satisfied at the cadence into m. 55, all the leaping about in this passage creates a sense of instability and undermines the sense of closure. Perhaps this is part of the reason for the short coda shown in Example 7.4 that ends the movement; it is coda from a Schenkerian perspective because it occurs after the main *Urlinie* descent has already been completed. This much more conventional ending gesture with its descending fifth from $\hat{5}$ to $\hat{1}$ reinforces the sense of closure in the obligatory register, compensating for the preceding instability. This is followed at the end of m. 59, however, by an ascending gesture. These four measures do not appear at the equivalent point in the A section of the Menuetto—Mozart has saved the idea until the end. As the first

Example 7.4 Mozart, String Quartet in C major, K. 465, Menuetto, mm. 56–end

violin trills up to the C at the end, it provides a final uplifting flourish, which could also be interpreted as a reference to the weak closure on the same note in m. 50. If mm. 56–9 stabilize the closure in the obligatory register, the next four measures could be understood as picking up on and reinforcing the hint of closure in the higher register.

The above analysis suggests an interpretation of the piece based upon interplay between three registers, each of which has a slightly different dramatic function. The E at the beginning of Example 7.2 is the point of departure, a default register in which the main descent to $\hat{1}$ takes place. The lower register represented by the F in m. 43 and D in m. 51, is the register of surprise and disjunction; there is no closure in this octave, instead the music both times has to work its way back up to the main register. The upper register, on the other hand, ultimately turns out to be a rival to the main register—the fleeting closure at m. 50 translates into a final triumphant flourish at the end. We can never really know how composers intend their music to be understood on such a detailed level but, as in a performance, an analysis is an interpretation. With the preceding series of graphs I invite you to understand the music in a particular way that might inform your hearing or performance of this movement. At the same time, and on a more theoretical level, my analysis attempts to show how the music is an elaboration of some very basic middleground progressions in the spirit of Schenker's motto of "always the same but not in the same way."

Menuetto from Beethoven's Piano Sonata in F minor, Op. 2, No. 1

The Menuetto from Mozart's quartet involves octave displacements of a simpler progression in the middleground, a very common feature even if not necessarily always foregrounded to this degree. In the Menuetto from Beethoven's Op. 2, No.1 Piano Sonata, however, the register transfer occurs in an inner part, which initiates interplay between the upper two voices.

From the point of view of the overall structure, Beethoven's Menuetto can be understood as a minor key variant of the same basic *Ursatz* pattern as the previous example. Example 7.5 shows how this background layer relates to the formal structure. The A section of the binary form movement moves from F minor not to the dominant but to III—A♭ being the relative major. The beginning of the B section then moves from relative major to dominant in preparation for a modified reprise of the A section. It is not, of course, the fact that you can reduce the movement to this basic archetype that is most interesting but what you learn about the details of the foreground by approaching them from this perspective.

Example 7.6 provides a middleground of the A section of the Menuetto, which basically prolongs $\hat{3}$ over an arpeggiation in the bass from I to III. The first four measures elaborate an unfolding in the upper voice from A♭ to C (marked with a heavy beam and stems in Example 7.6a). After an elaboration of C over the next six measures, a stepwise descent reverses the initial unfolding, arriving back on A♭ in m. 12. The whole figure therefore constitutes a reaching over—the C reaches over the A♭ ($\hat{3}$) and then descends by step onto it in m. 12. Another possible interpretation of this passage would be as a descent from $\hat{5}$.

The beginning of the subtle interplay between the upper two voices can be seen by comparing the phrase that starts on the upbeat to m. 7 with the succeeding phrase starting on the upbeat to m. 9. The second of these two phrases exactly repeats the previous two measures except that the alto voice E♭ (marked with a downward flag at the end of m. 7) is transferred up an octave to a higher E♭ so that it is now above the main melody (marked with an upwards flag at the end of m. 9). The crossing over of the two voices is marked with arrows in m. 9. The new upper voice persists until the F at the end of m. 10, which can be understood not only as a neighbor note to the E♭ but also as an anacrusis to the A♭ in m. 11. This A♭ represents a return to the register (and indeed the very note) with which the melody started. The disappearance of the upper voice at the end of the phrase is emphasized by the fact that the F neighbor in m. 10 is left hanging rather than resolving to an implied E♭ (shown in brackets in Example 7.6a). This

Example 7.5 *Ursatz* form for minor key binary form

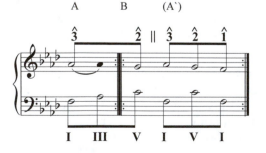

Example 7.6 Beethoven, Piano Sonata in F minor, Op. 2, No. 1, Menuetto, mm. 1–14

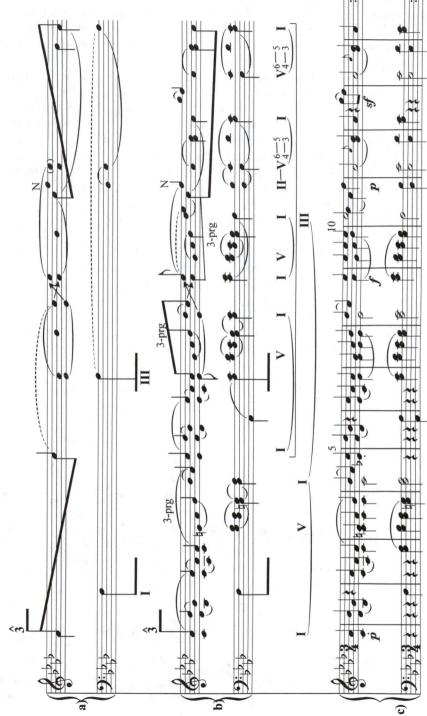

is further emphasized by the repetition of the closing gesture; attention is also drawn to the high F by the sforzando on this note the second time around at the end of m. 12. The apparently unfinished business of the alto voice and its register transfer is picked up in the recapitulation of this material.

The A section of the Menuetto is therefore on one level very simple—it decorates in various ways an A♭. At the same time, however, the way in which the alto voice leaps up above the melody ultimately sets up a striking juxtaposition of registers in the final section of the Menuetto. Subtle though the register transfer in the alto voice is, even this first section is open to dramatic interpretation. If one imagines the two parts as representing actors in a drama, the alto voice could be interpreted as making a bid for recognition or even dominance as it leaps up above the soprano. This anthropomorphic reading is, of course, highly fanciful, but such metaphors can be very helpful in conveying an interpretation and are certainly very much in the spirit of Schenker's own writing.

It is in the reprise of the A material, shown in Example 7.7, that the dramatic potential of the opening conflict between two voices is really exploited. In mm. 29–30 the melody from the beginning remains the same, but at the end of m. 29 a new idea comes in sforzando over the top. Although this is not literally a register transfer from the alto voice, it nevertheless strongly recalls the sequence of events in the first section. To continue with the dramatic interpretation suggested above, it is almost as

Example 7.7 Beethoven, Piano Sonata in F minor, Op. 2, No. 1, Menuetto, mm. 29–40

if the alto voice is not prepared to wait for its moment of prominence but instead jumps in early, over the top of the main melody. This moment is again marked with an arrow at the end of m. 29.

In the first section of the Menuetto, the register transfer had no real impact on the middleground structure of the music—the basic prolongation of Ab was unaffected. In the reprise, however, the sudden entry of the new voice at the end of m. 29 results in an emphatic descending fifth progression from $\hat{5}$ to $\hat{1}$ (from the end of m. 30 to the beginning of m. 36). From a Schenkerian point of view, this resolute closure would be a good candidate for the final descent were it not for the fact that it is in the "wrong" register; it is not, in other words, in the obligatory register established by the opening, which suggests a descent onto this lower F rather than the higher one in m. 36.

Beethoven does close in the original register two measures later by returning to the repeated cadential idea from the end of the A section. However, this pianissimo descent onto F is rather overshadowed by the previous cadence. The sense of deflation is reinforced by the even more stripped-down cadence in the following two measures, which concludes the Menuetto on an F that is an octave lower again. To return again to the dramatic interpretation from before, the interrupting alto voice's quest for prominence is successful, but it is a pyrrhic victory in that the Menuetto as result ends with something of a damp squib.

Schenkerian techniques help both to expose and to represent the subtle registral interplay of this movement. The significance of the foreground events can be highlighted by their relationship to the basic structure of the piece—the descent from Ab to F. The main features of my interpretation are shown in the middleground summary in Example 7.8. The new voice that originates in the alto in the first section is shown in small noteheads. As with the previous analysis, it is in the description and explanation of this structure that an interpretation comes to life; it is perfectly possible for a reader to infer much of what is significant and interesting from graphs alone, but a written commentary is an invaluable guide.

Example 7.8 Beethoven, Piano Sonata in F minor, Op. 2, No. 1, summary of movement

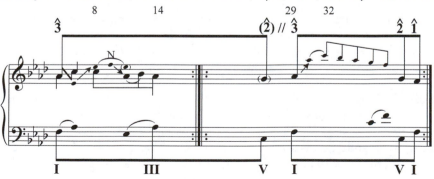

Chapter 8

Parallelisms and dramatic structure

Hidden repetition

The notion of a vast and infinitely various tonal repertoire underpinned by the same basic archetype is vital to Schenkerian analysis, but equally important is the idea of coherence and unity within individual pieces. The *Ursatz* embodies at least two different types of unity: first, there is a thread of continuity from $\hat{3}$ to $\hat{1}$ that theoretically draws a piece into a coherent whole; second, tonal works are unified simply because they are ultimately an elaboration of a single tonic. This second type of unity is perhaps less tangible—it cannot literally be traced through the work like linear unity—but this does not make it any less important to the concept of the *Ursatz*.

The *Ursatz* not only unifies a tonal work for Schenker but is also the ultimate source of all the musical form and content. Nevertheless, Schenker is also keen to emphasize the role of internal repetition. Musical repetitions occur both on the large scale, as in the exposition in the first movement of a symphony, and on the small scale, for example in the construction of melodies out of related motivic fragments. Schenker believes that this urge to repeat things in art comes from the natural world. In *Harmony*, his first theoretical treatise, he writes:

> Man repeats himself in man; tree in tree. In other words, any creature repeats itself in its own kind ... and by this repetition the concept "man" or "tree" is formed. Thus a series of tones becomes an individual in the world of music only by repeating itself in its own kind; and, as in nature in general, so music manifests a procreative [i.e. reproductive] urge, which initiates this process of repetition.[1]

Schenker's appeal to nature is part of his conviction that music should be organic; the term is used here to mean natural, developmental growth (like a plant from a seed), in opposition to mechanical construction. Like many composers and theorists of this period, Schenker believes that the best works of art are not just a collection of parts but that these parts make up a single and coherent interconnected whole. Motivic analysis appeals to the same idea by demonstrating how a piece of music has been developed organically out of its most basic melodic materials. Although Schenker sees the *Ursatz* as the ultimate source of musical unity, his conception of layers also allows him to add a whole new dimension to motivic analysis.

In *Free Composition* Schenker asserts that during the Baroque and Classical eras composers gradually became more sophisticated in the way they repeated material. Not only were motives developed and varied on the surface of the music, he suggests, but they begin to be found beneath the surface as well:

> New types of repetition then revealed themselves to composers of genius. Although these new types seem to lie just as clearly before the eye and ear as the repetitions that occurred within the imitative forms, they remained less accessible because they did not offer creator and listener the same ease of perception . . . it was precisely these concealed repetitions which freed music from the narrowness of strict imitation and pointed the way to the widest spans and most distant goals.[2]

This idea of "concealed repetition" (often called parallelism) is both intriguing and problematic. One assumption that it makes, for example, is that the densely motivic writing of composers such as Beethoven and Brahms is inherently superior to music that explores other creative paths. Schenker describes such composers—those, in fact, that provide the best examples for his theories—as geniuses. This allows him to suggest that concealed repetitions are not so much the product of compositional decisions as of unconscious inspiration—it might otherwise be hard to explain why, like most of his theoretical ideas, parallelisms are not mentioned by the composers he analyzes. Despite these issues, the concept of parallelism opens a fascinating field of analytical enquiry; I begin this chapter by discussing some of Schenker's own analyses before moving on to look at some examples of my own.

Schenker's analysis of Beethoven's Fifth Symphony (from the *Tonwille* series) provides a very clear example of what he means by concealed repetition.[3] The first movement of the Fifth Symphony is built on perhaps the most famous motive in western music—the falling major third with which the work opens. Schenker's analysis shows how the first two instances of this foreground motive (an unfolding of a third) can be understood as the decoration of an underlying neighbor note progression from E♭ to D as shown on Example 8.1a.[4] He goes so far as to assert that "it is not actually all four tones making up the principal motive that are of the essence, but merely the two half-notes separated by a step."[5] Schenker is not denying the significance of the falling third—that would be perverse—but his notion of concealed repetition opens up a whole new level on which this music can be understood in terms of motivic correspondences.

The next paragraph is shown in Example 8.1b, on which is marked the relentlessly repeating variants of the foreground X motive on which a traditional motivic analysis would probably focus. Schenker's analysis suggests, however, that the descending middleground neighbor note figure from the first five measures is also present. The chord built up by the entries of the X motive in mm. 6–10 is shown as an elaboration of the E♭ on the downbeat of m. 7, while the next series of entries prolong the D on the downbeat of m. 11. The whole eight-measure phrase can therefore be understood as an elaboration of a descending neighbor note from E♭ to D. In the next four

Example 8.1 Beethoven, Symphony No. 5, Allegro con brio: (a) Mm. 1–5;
(b) Mm. 6–21

Source: Based on Schenker 2004: 25–33

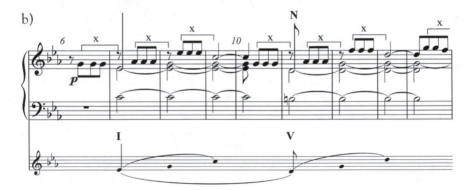

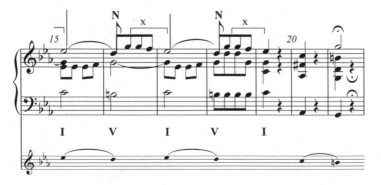

measures (mm. 15–18) this motive is repeated twice in the foreground, again over the same arpeggiation of I to V.

Schenker's analysis therefore shows how the repeating X motive decorates a larger-scale structure created by these descending neighbor notes. It is an analysis that makes plenty of intuitive sense, particularly because of the way in which the E♭s and Ds fall on accented beats and measures. With only a small effort, Schenker's neighbor-note idea can be heard in the first 21 measures almost as easily as the more obvious foreground motive from the first two measures.

In the above analysis of the first 21 measures of Beethoven's Fifth symphony, the many repetitions of the famous foreground motive are shown to be shaped and unified by the underlying neighbor note figures. This pattern itself is understood by Schenker as part of an even larger-scale series of descending linear motions across the whole movement.[6] The place of concealed repetition in relation to the overall structure of the *Ursatz* is much more easily seen in Schenker's analysis of Bach's Little Prelude in C major, which at only 16 measures is somewhat more easily grasped than the 502 measures of the first movement of Beethoven's Fifth.

Example 8.2a shows the opening six measures of the prelude, which, from the point of view of the *Ursatz*, elaborate a descent from $\hat{3}$ to $\hat{2}$. Schenker calls the rising fourth progression (motive Y) the "basic subject" of the piece, and it provides the basis for an eighth-note figuration over a tonic pedal. Like the neighbor note in the previous example, this rising fourth is easily audible, but it leads at the beginning of the fourth measure onto a C in an inner voice. Over the top of this culmination of the opening fourth progression enters the E that Schenker sees as the beginning of the *Urlinie*. Motive Y is therefore an elaboration of the initial tonic that ultimately supports the beginning of the main structural descent in m. 4.

The second repetition of this motive can be seen beginning at m. 9 in Example 8.2b, where the eighth-note figuration from the beginning returns. Whereas at the beginning motive Y elaborated the tonic, it here elaborates the dominant; the fourth progression picks up the D from m. 5 and ascends to G at the beginning of m. 12. Example 8.2c shows the final instance of motive Y, which is "veiled and accelerated" by the sixteenth notes in m. 14.[7] The rising fourth is harder to hear, because its elaboration in this case involves a register transfer between the second and third notes. Although the motive is less obvious, the eighth-note figuration begins in the same way as the previous examples, so Schenker's attempt to find a parallelism with these two passages seems reasonable. As at the beginning, the motive prolongs the tonic, but this time it supports the final $\hat{1}$ of the *Urlinie*. One way of understanding this analysis is that it seems to suggest that the concealed repetitions of the Y motive underpin much of the melodic content while the *Ursatz* provides the framework within which this unfolds.

Example 8.2 J. S. Bach, Little Prelude in C major, BWV 939: (a) Mm. 1–6; (b) Mm. 9–12; (c) Mm. 13–end

Source: Schenker 2004: 145

a)

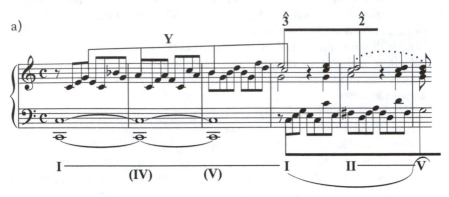

b)

c)

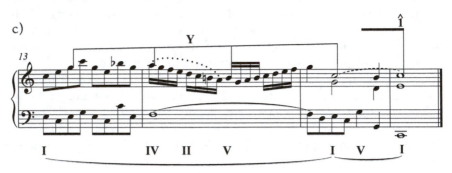

Beethoven, Piano Sonata in E major, Op. 14, No. 1

The recurrence of the rising fourth motive in the Little Prelude arises from the repetition of the foreground eighth-note figure. Although the parallelism with the final variation of this figure may not be deliberate, Schenker's analysis otherwise does little more than document the voice-leading structure of surface repetitions. It is more common for parallelisms to be less explicit than in this example; concealed repetitions usually link foreground figurations that are less obviously connected. Such analysis obviously has a rather more tenuous (and certainly less provable) link with the process of composition, showing how the piece *seems* to be unified by the concealed repetitions it reveals. This is the spirit in which the following analysis is offered, although it is worth pointing out that Schenker himself is rarely so modest about the status of his observations.

The first theme of Beethoven's Op. 14, No. 1 piano sonata consists of three simple ideas that seem relatively unconnected to each other: first, a series of rising pairs of half notes (see Example 8.3 below); second, a skittish two-beat sixteenth-note idea (Example 8.4); and, finally, a cadential phrase in which a two-measure rising arpeggiated eighth-note idea leads into a stepwise descent of two octaves (Example 8.5). The transition that follows begins with a modified reprise of the opening four measures (Example 8.6). In this analysis, I am interested in showing how each of these phrases can be understood to grow out of what has gone before. In looking for connections between ideas and developmental growth from one to another, I am adopting the analytical aesthetic discussed at the beginning of this chapter in promoting the idea of the musical work as a coherent whole.

As shown in Example 8.3 there is a small parallelism even within the first phrase of the movement. The foreground fourth-progression in the last measure is the same as the one that spans the whole first four measures in the tenor voice. This little melodic flourish in the right hand can thus be seen as a summary of the overall shape of the whole phrase. This shape is also outlined by the first two notes, which span the same fourth from B up to E.

If it seems a bit odd to suggest that these four measures are an elaboration of a progression in an inner voice, it is worth noting that the first three notes of this inner-voice progression are picked out on the first beat of each measure in the melody line as well (shown by the dotted lines on the example). In fact, it is the melodic flourish in the final measure that disrupts this pattern; the right hand ends instead on an E an octave higher than might be expected.

Example 8.3 Beethoven, Piano Sonata in E major, Op. 14, No. 1, Allegro, mm. 1–4

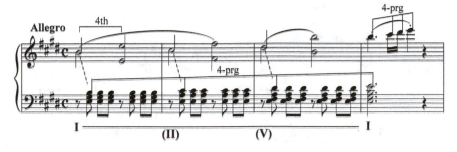

In my analysis of the opening of the sonata, I concentrate on the stepwise ascending fourth shown in the example, but this is of course only one aspect of the sonata. The series of rising pairs of half notes with which the piece begins becomes important later in the piece, reappearing prominently in the transition, coda and development as well as, of course, the recapitulation. I concentrate here, however, on the more subtle small-scale connections from one phrase to the next across the first theme.

Example 8.4 shows the next two measures of the sonata, which contrasts with the opening in terms of texture, motive and in the way in which it is broken up into much smaller phrases of two beats. Important as these contrasts are, there is also a connection between the two ideas in that they both contain stepwise ascents that span a fourth. Although the elaboration of this rising fourth is very different, one can still see how one might be understood to have grown out of the other. The fundamental difference is that whereas the first phrase involves a fourth progression, mm. 5 and 6 consist of a series of third progressions, the last note of which is decorated by an upper neighbor note.

The rest of the first subject (as seen in Example 8.5) turns out mostly to involve rising third progressions from G♯ to B, often in several voices at the same time. The eighth-note figure at m. 7 can be understood as a more expansive reworking of the sixteenth-note figures that begin in m. 5. Both decorate an ascending third progression from G♯ to B; the only fundamental difference is the lack of a neighbor note in the eighth-note figure. In this context, Example 8.4 can be understood to mediate between the music at the beginning (rising fourths) and that from m. 7 onwards (rising thirds) by incorporating both in its third-progression-plus-neighbor-note configuration.

After repeating the decorated rising third progression in m. 7 up an octave in the following measure, Beethoven balances this ascending motion with a stepwise descent of two octaves over the next three measures. However, as can be seen in Example 8.5, this descending passage retains a connection with what has happened previously through a series of ascending third progressions from G♯ to B in the inner voices. Two developments are

Example 8.4 Beethoven, Piano Sonata in E major, Op. 14, No. 1, Allegro, mm. 5–7

Example 8.5 Beethoven, Piano Sonata in E major, Op. 14, No. 1, Allegro, mm. 7–13

notable: first, the chromatic passing note A♯, which features prominently each time; second, the ascending thirds in mm. 9 and 11, which are balanced by the same third descending in mm. 10 and 12.

As shown in Example 8.6, the material from the beginning returns in m. 13, heralding the transition to the dominant key. In the light of the transformation of the initial rising fourth into an ascending third, followed by the addition of a chromatic passing note, it is fascinating that Beethoven re-writes the opening material so that it now consists of precisely this new idea. In both the tenor voice in mm.13–15 and in the melody from m. 15 onwards, the music outlines a rising third from G♯ to B with a chromatic passing note, A♯. It is as if the music has taken the ascending fourth from the opening, transformed it and then handed it back to the original theme in this changed form.

Example 8.6 Beethoven, Piano Sonata in E major, Op. 14, No. 1, Allegro, mm. 13–16

When considering this sort of subtle network of connections and transformations, it is easy to see why Schenkerians have often got carried away and described such connections as undeniable "facts" that their analysis has "uncovered." It is worth remembering that it would be surprising if we could not find passing-note progressions between G♯ and B in a piece in E major and that any move to the dominant is inevitably going to entail A♯ as the sharpened leading note. This is not to pour cold water on "concealed repetitions" but simply to warn that we should remain fully aware that an analysis is an interpretation of a particular aspect of the work, not the uncovering of an objective structure.

Beethoven, String Quartet in F minor, Op. 95

Schenkerian graphs are often used in order to help illustrate more general points of interpretation, not only to show the *Ursatz* or complex networks of detailed parallelisms. In the following analysis of the first movement of Beethoven's Op. 95 string quartet, the discussion draws on the Schenkerian concepts of layers and of concealed repetition; these are used, however, to support a more informal understanding of the movement than would be obtained by a fully developed Schenkerian analysis.

One of the notable features of the movement is that it compresses highly contrasting material into a comparatively short sonata form movement. As shown in Example 8.7b, the raw aggression of the opening five measures subsides unexpectedly quickly into the comparative calm of m. 7, out of which a rather more lyrical idea briefly emerges. The aggressive opening is firmly in the home key of F minor, but the escape from this turbulence from m. 6 seems to be strongly linked with a simultaneous flight to the relatively distant harmony of G♭ major.

From a Schenkerian perspective, this harmonic progression from tonic to flat II (Neapolitan) in m. 6 can be understood as generated by a linear event. The main bass note in the first five measures is F, which is prolonged by a move to its dominant (C), so the G♭ is therefore an upper neighbor note to the F, a relationship shown by the flagged stem in Example 8.7. If the top voice of the texture constitutes an unfolding from F up to C, then the neighbor note figure in the bass from F to G♭ seems to be mirrored by a similar neighbor note motion from C to D♭ in mm. 5–6. I am interested in how the intense dramatic contrasts of this movement continue to be mirrored in and supported by developments of this neighbor-note idea.

If you were trying to communicate these ideas with the expectation that your readers would be consulting a score, it would make more sense to summarize the analysis with a Schenkerian-type graph as in Example 8.7a. Accompanied by a little explanatory text, this middleground summary can economically show how the upper neighbor notes at m. 6 underpin the dramatic contrast between the turbulent opening and the calmer section

Example 8.7 Beethoven, String Quartet in F minor, Op. 95, Allegro con brio; mm. 1–7; (a) Analysis; (b) Short score

a)

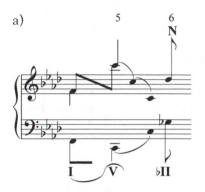

b)

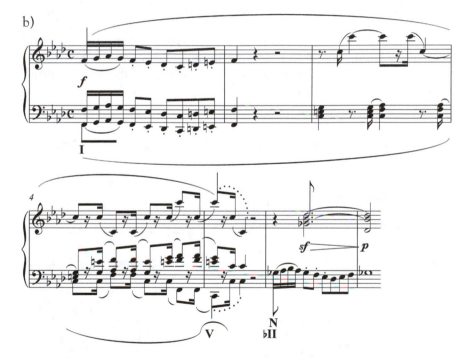

that follows. Readers can be left to resolve the details of such an analysis themselves.

The principal feature of the first seven measures from a linear perspective is a neighbor note that is strongly highlighted by its compositional setting. If the opening describes, therefore, a dramatic move from structural consonance of the tonic up to the structural dissonance of the Neapolitan neighbor notes, the passage that follows is dominated by neighbor note progressions that move in the opposite direction. As shown in Example 8.8, there is a series of descending neighbor notes, most of which exactly reverse the C to D♭ neighbor note from the top voice of the opening. This idea is most prominent in the first violin melody starting on the last beat of m. 12, but a detail from the previous two measures is worth noting. The second violin in m. 11 plays a dissonant D♭ (a ninth against the C major chord) that is left unresolved. In the next measure it moves up to a D♭ in the next octave but again it is unresolved. This time, however, it is picked up yet another octave higher by the first violin and finally resolves onto C on the first beat of m. 13. It seems to me that this resolution of D♭ onto C, along with the other descending neighbor notes in Example 8.8, is somehow an attempt to balance the dramatic semitone shift from I to ♭II in the first paragraph of the movement.

Example 8.9 shows the lead into the transition. The turbulent octave unison idea from the beginning returns, this time extended over three measures and culminating in a furious fortissimo in m. 20; as before, the mood of the music abruptly shifts in the following measure to something much more gentle and lyrical. The rising neighbor note from F to G♭ in the bass at the beginning was marked by a repetition of the opening figure in m. 6 (see Example 8.7). Here the same shift occurs much more quickly—

Example 8.8 Beethoven, String Quartet in F minor, Op. 95, Allegro con brio, mm. 9–15

Example 8.9 Beethoven, String Quartet in F minor, Op. 95, Allegro con brio, mm. 15–24

Incipit:

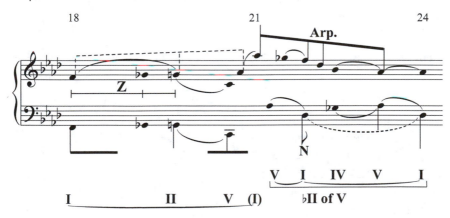

in the second half of m. 19. Rather than staying on G♭ as before, however, the music shifts up another semitone at the beginning of m. 20. I have called this extension of the G♭ neighbor-note idea motive Z, with its chromatic passing note between F and G (bracketed and labeled on Example 8.9).

This development of the G♭ neighbor-note idea into motive Z at m. 18 is foreshadowed in the viola part in mm. 15–17. The viola repeats a fragment from the opening figure starting on C and moving through D♭ to D, generating extra momentum into the cadence that ushers back in the opening idea. The emphatic arrival on C at the beginning of m. 21 is followed by another Neapolitan progression to ♭II, this time of the dominant. As before, the escape to tranquility is associated with an ascending neighbor note. The basic structure of the beginning of the transition is summarized by the graph on Example 8.9. The dotted stems and beams at the beginning show how the Z motive can be understood as part of a third progression in F minor. However, the tonic support for the A♭ never arrives as the music lurches straight into D♭ instead. Again this graph is primarily to show how the neighbor-note idea both develops but then is again associated with escape from turbulence into relative calm. A pattern has developed, then, in which the tonic is associated with turbulent aggression that is only dispelled when the music flees to a distant key.

As with the previous examples, I have only offered a snapshot of this movement in the hope that you will take this as a starting point for further study. In order fully to understand Example 8.10 you will need a score, but in essence it shows what happens to these ideas when the material is recapitulated towards the end of the movement. The recapitulation is extraordinarily condensed—starting at the equivalent of m. 18. Unlike in the exposition, the neighbor note D♭ resolves back to the dominant at around m. 93 as a preparation for what seems like a resolution to the tensions of

Example 8.10 Beethoven, String Quartet in F minor, Op. 95, Allegro con brio, mm. 82–99

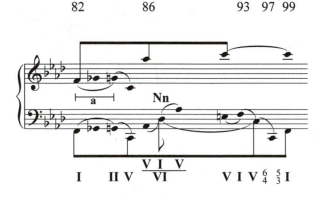

the movement so far. Whereas tranquility has been associated only with distant keys, at m. 99, it is associated with the tonic. This is, however, the tonic major, and you will see if you look at the rest of the movement that Beethoven saves plenty of drama for the coda.

Broadly, Schenkerian graphing techniques are widely used in the literature to illustrate analyses in which Schenker's notions of structure are not the main approach. As in the above examples, such analyses might not necessarily refer to deep middleground and background structures. In this analysis, I use Schenkerian notation to sharpen and clarify observations concerning motivic and dramatic structure. The ability to understand and produce such graphs is an invaluable skill for anyone interested in the analysis of tonal music.

Chapter 9

Beyond Schenker

The breakdown of tonal hierarchy

The tonal organization that Schenker describes is most relevant to the musical language exemplified by Haydn, Mozart and Beethoven; in fact, over 40 percent of the examples in *Free Composition* (Schenker's last major work) are taken from the music of these three composers alone. From this central repertory of Viennese masterworks, Schenker extends the scope of his enquiry back to Bach and Handel (together nearly 20 percent of the examples in *Free Composition*) and forwards to Brahms, Chopin and Schubert (around 30 percent).[1] With 80 percent of its examples taken from the music of just eight composers, *Free Composition* is not a comprehensive portrait of tonality across the ages; it is instead a detailed description of a very particular style, one that maintains a hugely important position in musical culture today.

A key feature of the language of this repertoire is the complex network of hierarchical relationships that it conjures up. These operate at every musical layer: in the foreground a neighbor note is subordinate to the pitch it elaborates, and in the deep background everything can ultimately be shown to be subordinated to the power of the tonic chord. Music theorists have used a wide range of metaphors to describe and explain the place of the tonic chord in the tonal system. Joseph Riepel, for example, writing in the 1770s, compared the hierarchical relationships between diatonic triads to those established on a farm.[2] Riepel suggested that the tonic was like the master, exercising control over his subordinates in the farm hierarchy; the dominant was compared to an overseer, while the subdominant was merely a laborer. Bizarre though this may seem, one can understand how the confident clarity of Example 9.1 might be heard as reflecting a harmonious social order. Riepel was one of several theorists who called upon similar metaphors in the second half of the eighteenth century.

The beginning of "Frightening" from Schumann's *Scenes of Childhood* (Example 9.2) begins with a much less certain sense of tonal order—the tonic only starts to crystallize in the third and fourth measures. The music's connection to the tonic is stretched like an elastic band before contracting back into place. And when such digressions from the diatonic harmony become more extended, there is a need for a different sort of metaphor.

Example 9.1 Haydn, Piano Sonata in F major, Hob. XVI, No. 23, Allegro

F: I   V   I IV I   I   V   I

Those interested in chord function (as opposed to Schenker's scale-based approach) have tended to use the language of geography to describe journeys around the networks of chord and key relations that have been mapped out by theorists such as Hugo Riemann.[3] This type of metaphor is the most common in informal analytical approaches: the tonic is "home," modulations are "excursions" and keys that are not closely related are "distant regions."

The complex networks of chromatically related keys in the work of composers such as Wagner, Mahler or Bruckner are less susceptible to Schenker's diatonic scale-based approach; it is certainly not so easy to hear works by these composers in terms of Schenker's *Ursatz* model, in which everything is ultimately subordinate to the tonic. The musical grammar, at least on the large scale, is therefore different to that of the Classical era and Schenker's theory in its purest form arguably describes it less well. This should not perhaps be too surprising given that he had serious reservations about the validity of this sort of music.[4]

Schenker's focus on music that has its foundations in the clear I–V–I diatonic structures of the Classical era means that he is also less interested in dissonant chords than other harmonic theorists. For him, only the triad is a true harmony; more complicated chords such as ninths and elevenths are not harmonic phenomena, but the result of interactions of contrapuntal lines.[5] His theory does not attempt to account for composers who, although

Example 9.2 Schumann, *Scenes of Childhood*, Op. 25, "Frightening"

(G: I   V   I   V)

their language is basically tonal, are interested in the sonorities created by extending the language of music beyond triads. The evocative dissonances of Debussy's prelude "The Sunken Cathedral" (Example 9.3) are quite outside the scope of Schenker's (although not necessarily Schenkerian) enquiry.

One way in which Schenkerian theory can nevertheless be useful for music that pushes the boundaries of the tonal repertoire is by providing a benchmark of standard tonal structure against which to measure the music being analyzed. The question becomes not "how can this piece be understood as an elaboration of the *Ursatz*?" but "in what ways does this piece diverge from traditional harmony and voice-leading practices as described by Schenkerian theory?" The following analysis of the Arabeske from Carl Nielsen's *Fem Klaverstyyker* (1890) offers a modest example of this approach. At the end of this short piano piece, shown in Example 9.4, both key signature and final chord suggest a tonic of D major, but the sense of this key is undermined in several ways.

On a very simple level, the way the chords are voiced in the final cadence are quite weak—a last inversion dominant seventh resolving onto a first inversion tonic. The previous harmonies also muddy the water considerably: in the first bar of the extract a dominant seventh resolves not onto I but onto chord III with a sharpened third. A speculative analysis of the harmonic and contrapuntal structure is offered above the staff in Example 9.4. The final bar represents the $\hat{1}/I$ expected by Schenker at the close of a piece, but not only is the dominant approach not very emphatic in its voicing but neither is there a clear $\hat{2}$ or even a leading note $\hat{7}$ leading onto the $\hat{1}$. The closest is the C♯ in the second bar of the extract, but this is harmonized not by the dominant but by III♯.

There are similar ambiguities at the beginning of the piece as shown in Example 9.5, which opens with the same V–III♯ pattern already encountered. If the ending is tonally ambiguous, this opening is far more so; the music moves from the dominant seventh at the beginning through III♯ arriving in the sixth measure on D♯ minor.

Example 9.3 Debussy, *Preludes*, Book I, No. 10 ("The Sunken Cathedral")

Example 9.4 Nielsen, *Five Pieces for Piano*, Op. 3, "Arabeske," mm. 31–end

Again, I present an attempt to account for the voice-leading in Schenkerian terms above the staff. By the time there is any hint of a *Kopfton*—the $\hat{3}$ in the sixth measure—the harmony is a long way from the tonic. The attempt to show an initial arpeggiation in this example is problematic, because the rising arpeggio of A, C♯ and F♯ is hard to reconcile to a larger-scale harmonic unit.

The piece seems ultimately to hover between D major and F♯ major and one can find further hints of both these keys at various points in the piece. Example 9.6 shows a moment about halfway through when the music seems to hint strongly at the dominant of D major, although the apparent suspended fourth never resolves.

Example 9.5 Nielsen, *Five Pieces for Piano*, Op. 3, "Arabeske," mm. 1–8

A little later, however, the music veers towards the alternative pole of F♯ minor, as shown in Example 9.7 with some tentative stabs at a perfect cadence in this key.

There is in fact a programmatic reason for all this harmonic ambiguity that is suggested by the first two lines of a Jacobsen poem that Nielsen quotes at the top of the *Arabeske*: "Have you lost your way in the darkening forest? Do you know Pan?" After the initial dominant seventh in m. 1 the music does indeed seem to "lose its way"; the continued turns to F♯ represent a "wrong" turn that is finally made "right" at the end.

Example 9.6 Nielsen, *Five Pieces for Piano*, Op. 3, "Arabeske," mm. 13–14

Example 9.7 Nielsen, *Five Pieces for Piano*, Op. 3, "Arabeske," mm. 19–21

Although this can be described reasonably satisfactorily without Schenkerian analysis, a graph helps to sharpen up our understanding of the extent to which this piece conforms (or otherwise) to "normal" tonal structures as represented by the *Ursatz*. As can be seen in Example 9.8, there is the semblance of an interrupted descent from 3̂, but it takes quite an act of will to hear the piece in this way. The substitution (shown in brackets towards the end) and the very weak and ambiguous harmonic underpinning for all of the *Urlinie* tones mean that the *Ursatz* is more of a shadow in the background than a firm tonal framework within which the piece unfolds.

As shown in Example 9.9, Franz Liszt's "Nuages Gris" (1881) pushes the boundaries of tonality further than the Nielsen example; the ambiguity of the music again has programmatic origins this time suggested by the title, which translates as "Grey Clouds." The voice-leading of the first six bars

Example 9.8 Nielsen, *Five Pieces for Piano*, Op. 3, "Arabeske"

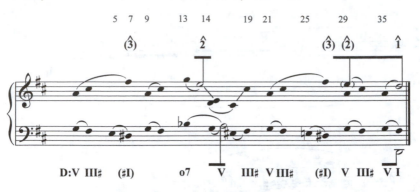

Example 9.9 Liszt, "Nuages Gris," S. 199, mm. 1–6

suggests (but certainly does not confirm) the tonality of G minor, with a C♯ chromatic neighbor note that resolves onto D.

A little later in the piece (as shown in Example 9.10) there are again hints of G minor, with even a hint of a I–V–I structure hidden beneath the dissonances and ambiguities. The way in which lines converge on the G minor harmony in the last bar of this extract is quite compelling, but the counterpoint along the way is rather harder to make sense of in terms of this tonality.

As shown in Example 9.11, the linear structure of the end of "Nuages Gris" suggests the possibility of G minor much less convincingly as the outer voices move in contrary motion towards G. The bass never arrives on G, however, and the harmony undermines any possible resolution as the tonal sense of the music and the piece itself seem to disappear into obscurity, as if into the grey clouds. The chord at the end sounds more like a heavily inflected dominant of D than anything else.

Example 9.10 Liszt, "Nuages Gris," S. 199, mm. 25–8

Example 9.11 Liszt, "Nuages Gris," S. 199, mm. 41–end

If in the Nielsen "Arabeske" the harmonic structures integral to *Ursatz* become obscured, in the Liszt we begin to lose our sense of tonal hierarchy altogether. Although the lines may suggest some sort of harmonic goal, this is not music in which a strict hierarchy of tones can be observed. In the Nielsen the unifying power of the *Ursatz* is severely tested, but it is still useful to approach this piece with the Schenkerian model more or less intact, allowing us to discover the ways in which Nielsen resists conformity to the standard structures that this model proposes. In the Liszt, however, while Schenker's ideas on contrapuntal structure seem to have some relevance, his model of the background is less helpful.

Felix Salzer, one of Schenker's pupils, argued strongly that the basic principles of Schenker's ideas on structure could be applied far beyond the realm of the tonal music with which Schenker himself was concerned. Salzer's analysis of the slow movement from Bartok's fifth string quartet in Example 9.12 shows his approach very clearly.

Salzer retains the idea of multilayered contrapuntal elaboration, but radically extends the way in which the hierarchies of the tonal system might operate. Rather than relying on the power of the I–V–I axis, Salzer allows hierarchies based solely on the linear structure of the piece in hand to emerge. This is most easily explained by choosing a note in the piece and tracing back the hierarchical relationships shown in Salzer's graph.

Example 9.12 Bartók, String Quartet No. 5, as analyzed in Felix Salzer's *Structural Hearing*

Source: Salzer 1982: Figure 452

a)

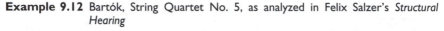

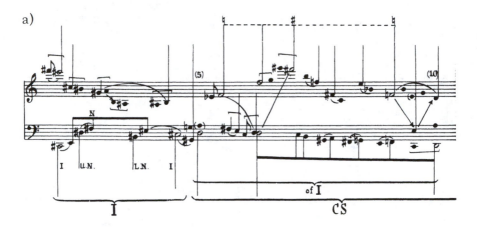

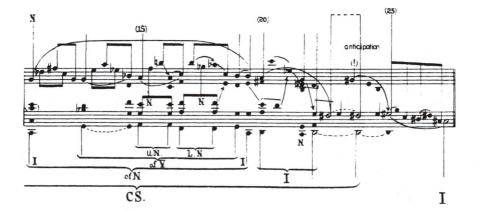

If we take the A in the bass in m. 15 as our starting point, we can see that Salzer suggests that it belongs in a complex hierarchical network. The A is an upper neighbor to the preceding G, which is itself the dominant of C that starts halfway through m. 10. This C is in turn a neighbor note to the D in the previous measure, and this D, whose elaboration stretches from m. 10 right through to m. 25, is ultimately a neighbor note to the C♯ that begins and ends this section. The principle is superficially similar to the way a Schenkerian analysis works, but this nested set of relationships does not rely in the same way on a pre-existing hierarchy of tonic/dominant relationships.

It could be argued, however, that the notion of a whole piece centered around a I–V–I structure breaks down in music much earlier than Bartók. Lawrence Kramer has discussed how the tonal structures of Classical pieces are large-scale projections of tonic/dominant relationships that also govern the foreground syntax. He further suggests that this "mirror" relationship between surface "presentation" and monotonal (diatonic) "horizon" is broken in the Romantic era as the foreground becomes ever more complex in the music of composers such as Bruckner and Mahler.[6]

An even more serious challenge, at least from a Schenkerian perspective, is if the background of a work no longer articulates a closed I–V–I structure. Schenker analyzes several such pieces in *Free Composition*, most of which begin and end in fifth-related keys. If the tonally closed *Ursatz* is the source of all unity and coherence, such pieces present a difficulty, related not so much to methodology as to aesthetics.

Schenker formulates a general exception to cover Chopin's second Op. 28 Prelude (beginning in E minor and finishing in A):

> Even though the bass form which begins with I is the only true image of the fundamental structure, the bass can, if the synthesis requires, occasionally start with the V, provided a fifth-progression in the upper voice defines the specific harmony.[7]

In the case of Chopin Mazurka Op. 30, No. 2 (B minor—F♯ minor), however, he can only say in with some bewilderment that "the uncertainty which rises about the tonality . . . almost prevents us from calling this Mazurka a completed composition."[8]

While beginning and ending in different keys may apparently be a Schenkerian theoretical bombshell, in the context of other threats to Classical tonality and form, it registers, in reality, as a fairly mild disruption. William Benjamin prefers to locate the main challenge in a fundamental shift that occurs during the latter half of the nineteenth century in music that is apparently unproblematic from this point of view: "the fact of beginning and ending in the same key may lead to an experience only of *return to*, and not of *motion within* or *prolongation of*, that properly speaking constitutes monotonality."[9] In other words, Benjamin is suggesting the complex tonal structures of late Romantic composers are difficult to understand in terms of the *Ursatz*, whether they begin and end on the same tonic chord or not.

Many scholars since Salzer have adapted Schenker's analytical models for use with music that either stretches the limits of common practice tonality or abandons it altogether. Anything that goes against the fundamental simplicity of Schenker's model of elaborative growth from tonic chord to foreground disrupts the whole ecology of his theory. The only danger is failing to acknowledge this fact; the moment we start to adapt Schenkerian thought we need to re-think and evaluate the sort of analytical questions that we ask and the context within which we are asking them.

It is just as important to be clear what sort of questions we are trying to answer when analyzing the firmly tonal repertoire at the center of Schenker's interests. In tracing a hypothetical growth from background to foreground, we inevitably concentrate on some qualities of the music at the expense of others.

Approaching a piece of music with *Ursatz* in hand means embracing an aesthetic that places particular value on such things as organic growth and unity. Schenker's vision of music as the miraculous transformation of a simple contrapuntal and harmonic structure is an integral part of his analytical method. One of the things that makes his work so fascinating is the way in which this clear aesthetic and philosophical vision is combined with an unlimited appetite for exploring detail.

A Schenkerian analysis is excellent at explaining how a piece is unified as an elaboration of the tonic or how it can be understood to introduce or resolve large-scale linear tensions. It reveals rather less about the way in which, for example, different rhythms or references to contrasting styles or genres are brought into conflict. Schenker's approach is only one of many possible ways of exploring a piece of tonal music, but it is nevertheless a richly rewarding one.

Part IV

Exercises

The first two groups of exercises (A and B) present short foreground and middleground extracts respectively as an introduction to the methodology of Schenkerian analysis. These extracts are short enough that they should be presented aligned with the music—this should be done either using a music publishing package, such as Sibelius or Finale, or neatly and carefully by hand. Further tips on completing these exercises as well as a summary of completing analyses using music publishing software can be found on www.SchenkerGUIDE.com, along with some even shorter drill-type exercises.

Group C presents extracts of longer works in order to build up a picture of larger-scale structures, while Group D offers shorter passages that present particularly interesting analytical problems. Finally, the exercises in Group E involve reconciling Schenker's own analyses from *Free Composition* to the details of the music.

Foreground analysis

These exercises are for practicing stages one and two of the analytical method discussed in Chapter 4. Complete a harmonic analysis first and then prepare a graph on which immediate elaborations of those harmonies are identified. Remember that the neighbor notes, arpeggiations and linear progressions must make sense of the harmony they elaborate. Remember to keep an eye out for compound melody and elaborations in combination, resulting in reaching over and other more complex embellishments.[1]

Foreground analysis should be fairly straightforward and you should initially avoid complicating things by trying to find larger-scale progressions. Nevertheless, you should use your common sense in not analyzing absolutely every vertical arrangement of notes as a harmony on its own. In Exercise A2, for example, it does not really make sense to identify three distinct chords in the second measure. On the other hand, a foreground harmony will sometimes be implied without there being clear support in the bass. A good example of this is in the first measure of Exercise A11, in which the implied harmony clearly changes on the last quarter of the measure. Once you have completed your foreground analysis, it is worth trying to find middleground connections beneath the surface.

A1: from Haydn, Hob. XVI, No. 5, Variation 2

A2: from Haydn, Hob. XVI, No. 40/II

Note: The second measure is probably better understood as a single harmony (in the same way that the chord remains the same in the last beat of the previous measure).

A3: from Mozart, KV 103, No. 5, Trio

Note: Chromatic passing notes are extra decorations rather than creating linear progressions in the Schenkerian sense.

A4: from Corelli, Violin Sonata, No. 6, Allegro

Note: Watch out for elaborations in the bass—just because it is moving at half the speed does not mean that every eighth represents a new harmony.

A5: from Mozart, KV 103, No. 12, Trio

Note: Watch out for compound melody in the bass.

A6: from Mozart, KV 103, No. 9, Minuet

Note: Avoid cluttering up your analysis with consecutive repeated notes.

A7: from Schubert, Op. 42, Andante poco moto

A8: from Mozart, KV 103, No. 11

A9: from Mozart, KV 15, No. 2

A10: from Mozart, KV 15, No. 6

A11: from Haydn, Hob. XVI, No. 10

Note: Do not let the spread chords put you off; the basic structure of the melody is fairly straightforward.

A12: from Mendelssohn, "Song without words"

A13: from Haydn, Hob. IX, No. 12, Minuet 3

Note: The concept of compound melody is helpful in this exercise.

A14: from Mozart, KV 315, No. 1

Note: A compound melody does not necessarily imply the same number of voices consistently throughout a passage.

A15: from Chopin, Op. 56, No. 1

Note: This passage begins not with a compound melody but with two different types of elaboration working in combination.

A16: from Mozart, KV 15, No. 3

A17: from Mozart, KV 15, No. 22

A18: from Mozart, KV 15, No. 4

Note: Peeking into the middleground is also helpful in this exercise. What is the basic underlying shape behind this extract?

Middleground analysis

In these short middleground exercises, you should be able to find one or two main underlying elaborations upon which the extracts are based. The first six are all cadential passages and can be understood as miniature realizations of the *Ursatz*, complete with a descending line and I–V–I *Bassbrechung*. You will find that each one presents a slightly different challenge in the way it elaborates the *Ursatz*.

B1: from Mozart, KV 103, No. 4, Trio

B2: from Mozart, KV 103, No. 3, Trio

B3: from Haydn, Hob. XVII, No. 3, Variation I

Note: Watch out for unfoldings and do not be put off by the sudden introduction of an additional voice at the end of the first full measure.

B4: from Mozart, KV 15, No. 1

Note: Although linear progressions that directly elaborate the *Ursatz* should not introduce new voices above the *Urlinie* (see discussion on pp. 65–8), this does not mean that foreground elaborations of middleground descents such as those in these examples cannot drop down (or reach over) onto the notes of the underlying progression.

B5: from Haydn, Hob. IX, No. 11, Minuet No. 4, Trio

Note: You may have to work a little harder to make this one fit to Schenker's descending archetype.

B6: from Mozart, KV 264, Theme

B7: from Mozart, KV 353, Theme

Note: A single elaboration underpins this short passage.

B8: from Corelli, Violin Sonata No. 10, Gavotta

Note: Although a single elaboration underpins this extract, think carefully how the last note relates to this elaboration.

B9: from Mozart, KV 103, No. 12, Trio

Note: A middleground progression near the surface such as this will not necessarily have all of its notes equally supported harmonically.

B10: from Haydn, Hob. I, No. 85, Trio

Note: This extract contains more than one main middleground progression.

B11: from Mozart, KV 103, No. 1, Trio

Note: As in some of the exercises in Group A, the top voice of this compound melody is not necessarily the most important.

B12: from Mozart, KV 33b

B13: from Haydn, Hob. 17, No. 2, Theme

Note: The basic structure of this extract has some similarities to Exercise B8.

B14: from Haydn, Hob. I, No. 85, Menuetto

Note: The fifth full measure is the trickiest of this extract—think carefully which note from the underlying progression it elaborates.

Group C

Longer extracts

This group of exercises provide several extracts from a longer movement as a way into the larger-scale structure. In most cases, there are suggestions for further work with the score.

C1: Handel, Suite for Harpsichord in B♭ Major, HW 434, Air and variations

a)

b)

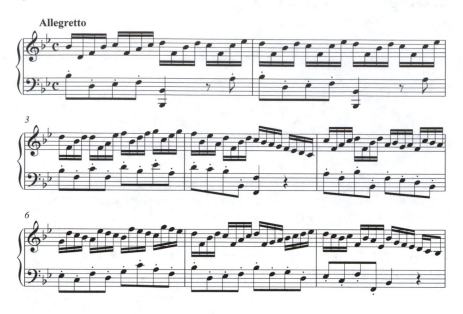

Notes:

1   C1a shows the Air on which this set of variations by Handel is based. Think about the overall *Ursatz* structure of this theme. Is it a single descent or an interruption? Does it begin on the *Kopfton* or is there an initial arpeggiation or ascent?

2   C1b shows the first variation. The right hand implies more than one voice here—try to show all the voices on your analysis. A first glance might suggest parallel fifths in the sixth measure of this variation once the voices are folded back together. How can this measure be represented so that the underlying structure is not parallel fifths?

3   C1c shows the second variation. Again, there are some interesting things going on here in terms of multiple voices. What is the relationship between the first four measures and the second four from this point of view?

c)

C2: Mozart, Eight Menuette, KV 315, No. 1

a)

b)

Notes:

1   C2a shows the Menuet section. Is this a single descent or an interruption? Is the *Kopfton* $\hat{3}$ or $\hat{5}$? Avoid the temptation to locate the whole of the final descent in the final few measures—often such descents are a foreground duplication of a larger-scale descent.

2   C2b shows the Trio section, which in the first instance you should analyze as a self-contained structure. You will notice that the first section does not move to the dominant, so you are not going to find an interruption at this point. It is quite common to find a complete descent across this type of tonic A section, which will ultimately be treated as a subsidiary linear progression that prolongs the *Kopfton* (see Example 4.7).

3   Show the structure of the whole piece using a middleground summary—remember that the Menuet is reprised after the Trio. How does the local *Kopfton* of the Trio affect your view of the overall *Kopfton* of the Menuet?

C3: Mozart, Sonata in C major, KV 545, Andante

a)

b)

Notes:

1   C3a shows the first section of this Andante from Mozart's famous C
major sonata, which you should treat as a self-contained structure in
the first instance. Is this a descent from $\hat{3}$ or $\hat{5}$.

2   C3b shows the next section, which leads back to a shortened reprise of
the opening. What is the main structural note being prolonged in this
section? Does this change your decision as to the *Kopfton* from 1)?

3   C3c shows a minor key section at mm. 33–48. Treat this as a self-
contained structure first, thinking carefully about the prolongation of
the *Bassbrechung* (m. 40 is a key moment in this regard).

4   Turning to the score, look at the section from m. 62. What is the
structure and function of this passage?

5   Provide a middleground summary of the whole movement, showing
how it all fits together. Write a short commentary explaining the key
decisions you have made and why.

c)

C4: Beethoven, Piano Sonata in A major, Op. 2, No. 2, Largo

a)

b)

Notes:

1   C4a shows the first eight measures of the second movement of a Beethoven piano sonata. Think about how you would analyze this extract if it was a whole piece—it follows one of the most common prolongations of the *Ursatz*.

2   C4b shows mm. 13–19, which can again be understood in terms of a small-scale descent. The changes of register prevent it being an orthodox *Ursatz* pattern that could span a whole piece.

3   Turning to the score, the passage that follows C4b (second half of m. 19 to m. 31) is probably the trickiest of this movement. You need to think carefully about what the main voice is at different points and how the music leads back into the repeat of the opening material at m. 32.

4   The rest of the movement involves further modified repeats of the material in C3a interspersed with some new material. Take each section separately, but keep in mind how the interspersed material prepares for the reprises in each case.

5   Show the overall structure of the movement using a middleground summary, along with a short commentary noting any points of interest.

C5: Schubert, Sonata in G major, Op. 78, Menuetto

a)

b)   **Allegro Moderato**

Notes:

1   C5a shows the reprise of the first section of the Menuetto (mm. 35 to 52), which you should first of treat as a self-contained structure. The main issue is *Kopfton*, which could be either $\hat{3}$ or $\hat{5}$. The prolongation of the *Bassbrechung* involves a heavily emphasized third divider. You also need to think carefully about voices and register in the second half of this passage.

2   C5b shows the first part of the Menuetto, of which C5a is a modified reprise. The concept of third divider is again important, but how is the D major prolonged locally and how does this impact (if at all) on the decision you have already made about the *Kopfton* in C5a?

3   Turning to the score, look at the passage that links C5a and C5b. Sometimes such passages take the music to the dominant in readiness for the reprise, but this is not the case here. What is the function of this passage in relation to the overall *Ursatz* structure?

4   Look at the trio section, considering carefully the roles of the various upper voices and their function as an interpolation between the Menuetto and its repeat.

5   Produce a middleground summary and commentary explaining the overall form of the movement.

C6: Haydn, Sonata in A♭ Major, Hob. XVI, No. 43, Moderato)

Notes:

1 C6 shows the recapitulation from the first movement of a Haydn piano sonata. Bear in mind that, if this follows the expected pattern, it will consist of an *Urlinie* descent that spans the whole passage.

2 Turning to the score, there are 21 measures after the end of C6, which implies that the rest of the movement might be a coda. See if you can disprove this by extending the final descent to later in the movement, then see if you can show how the material from m. 127 might be an elaboration of the final $\hat{1}$.

3 Analyze the exposition. How does this differ to the recapitulation analyzed in C6?

4 Produce a graph that shows what happens in the development. This is quite tricky—try to work out how this section can be understood as an expansion of the dominant with which it begins and ends.

5 Produce a middleground summary and commentary explaining the overall form of the movement.

C7: Mozart, Sonata in C, KV 330, Allegro moderato

a)

Notes:

1   C7a shows the second subject recapitulation (mm. 110–21). Getting this passage right is the key to this whole movement—treat it as a self-contained problem for the moment. Is it a plausible *Urlinie* descent from 5̂ (i.e. properly supported)? If not, it is likely to be a descent from 3̂. Do not be put off by the excursions into a higher register.

2   C7b shows the opening (mm. 1–18). What is the *Kopfton* here? The discussions towards the end of Chapter 6 will be helpful in thinking about this problem.

3   Turning to the score, the passage from m. 19 is the equivalent to C7a. Check to see if there are any major differences and then see how it can be understood as a continuation of C7b.

4   Show how the passage from m. 129 (and its equivalent in the recapitulation) can be understood as a series of closing gestures after the main descent to 1̂.

b)

5   Most of the development is reasonably straightforward harmonically, but the notion of linear intervallic progressions might help you work out what is happening in the slightly trickier passage from m. 71.

6   Produce a middleground summary and commentary explaining the overall form of the movement.

C8: Haydn, Sonata in E major, Hob. XVI, No. 22, Allegro moderato

Notes:

1 C8 shows the first part of the recapitulation (mm. 42–60), which takes us to $\hat{2}$ of the structural descent of the *Urlinie*. Each note of the *Urlinie* is quite substantially prolonged—this is not one of the descents that happens all at once at the end.

2 Turning to the score, look at mm. 60 to the end. Where would you locate the structural $\hat{1}$? If you are looking for a local reinforcing descent, you might find the concept of substitution helpful. The diminished sevenths are quite tricky to interpret in this passage—it is probably a good idea to leave them until last.

3 Look at the exposition. Presuming that most of the material is interpreted in broadly the same way, what is going on terms of the *Ursatz* in this section?

4 The approach to the recapitulation at m. 42 is really very unusual. Have a go at finding the main scale-steps that lead back to I and how they are elaborated. The chord at m. 36 is an augmented sixth onto D♯ major (the dominant of G♯ minor).

5 Produce a middleground summary and commentary explaining the overall form of the movement.

C9: Haydn, Sonata in C major, Hob. XVI, No. 48, Rondo

a)

b)

Notes:

1   C9 shows the Rondo theme from this Haydn movement. Remember that a descent from $\hat{5}$ must be supported throughout both contrapuntally and harmonically—if such support cannot be found, a descent from $\hat{3}$ is a better analysis. If the second six measures are an elaborated repeat of the first, how might this affect your analysis of the *Ursatz* structure?

2   Turning to the score, identify the reprises of this Rondo theme—note and analyze any differences.

3   Look at the intervening episodes and work out how they work their way back to the reprises of the Rondo material.

4   Produce a middleground summary and commentary explaining the overall form of the movement.

C10: Chopin, Mazurka, Op. 68, No. 3

Notes:

1   C10 shows the opening of this mazurka. The *Ursatz* does not necessarily progress at an even pace—remember that all the notes of the descent need proper support and watch out for displaced $\hat{2}$s at the cadences.
2   Turning to the score, work out how the piece proceeds from this opening and how the various intervening sections relate to this material.

Group D

Problematic extracts

These exercises pose various problems from the point of view of background analysis. Some of these are more easily surmounted than others and in solving them you will both understand a little more about how to reconcile pieces to Schenker's *Ursatz* model and also have the opportunity to reflect on its advantages and disadvantages. For each exercise, you should write a commentary that explains how you have reconciled the piece to the Schenkerian model and also discuss to what extent this leads to a useful analysis of the piece in question.

D1: Brahms, Waltz, Op. 39, No. 5

Note: The beginning and end of this Brahms waltz are analyzed in Chapter 3 (see Example 3.33). This analysis suggests that the principal action occurs in the alto voice. Flesh out this idea by showing how the journey from $\hat{3}$ to $\hat{1}$ might be prolonged. You will find that this in itself is not unproblematic—can you suggest any alternative readings? What are their advantages and disadvantages?

D2: Mozart, Menuetto, KV 176, No. 1

Notes: It is hard to see how this little menuetto can be understood in terms of a descent. Try to make it fit by employing the notion of register transfer while ignoring the principle of obligatory register. Can you come up with an alternative *Urlinie*-type structure? What are the advantages/disadvantages of these different approaches?

D3: Mozart, Twelve Minuets, KV 103, No. 1

Notes: In the final six measures, which should be analyzed first, there is a reasonably straightforward choice between a descent from $\hat{3}$ and $\hat{5}$. Whichever you choose, mm. 21–2 are simply a repetition down the octave of the previous two measures. The register changes in the first half of the minuet are more troublesome from the point of view of the *Urlinie*, but there is an orthodox solution to the problem.

D4: Schubert, Die Schöne Müllerin, "Der Müller und der Bach"

Notes: The structure of this extract from Schubert's famous song cycle presents an interesting problem with its prominent Neapolitans (♭II). You should be able to show the whole extract as a single prolongation of the *Ursatz*. Any doubt you may have about the *Kopfton* at the beginning should be dispelled by the central section.

D5: Beethoven, Piano Sonata in G major, Op. 14, No. 2, Andante

Notes: Think carefully before deciding on the *Kopfton* for this theme. There is a potential problem of register as well as whether the descent is from $\hat{3}$ or $\hat{5}$. Is the main register represented in mm. 13–16 or 17 to the end?

D6: Beethoven, Variations on a Waltz by Diabelli, Op. 120

2

Notes: Complete an analysis of this theme in terms of the *Ursatz*. You will find the concept of unfolding useful for your analysis. Discuss the extent to which the *Ursatz* provides useful model for this theme—can you suggest any alternative structure?

D7: Beethoven, Piano Sonata in D major, Op. 10, No. 3, Menuetto and Trio

Notes: This movement is quite problematic in terms of the *Ursatz*—it would make a good springboard for a discussion of what a Schenkerian analysis can tell us. If you are minded to be critical of Schenker's model in relation to this piece, think carefully first about whether there is anything about the music that the analytical difficulties might in fact highlight. Do not neglect the middle voices (e.g. at m. 25). You might want to find a score of the work and see how the Trio fits into the structure of the movement as a whole.

D8: Daquin, Le Coucou

Notes: At first glance this looks reasonably straightforward, but the problem is the relationship between the two voices represented by B at the beginning of the first measure and the G at the beginning of the second. Tracing either of these down through a fully supported descent in the correct register is quite a challenge. Try to come up with a solution that involves taking first one then the other voice as a starting point: what are the merits of these two interpretations?

D9: Chopin, Mazurka, Op. 67, No. 2

Incipit:

Notes:

1 Analyze the first 16 measures. They may not look tricky at first, but there are two problems: first, that it is hard to locate $\hat{2}$–$\hat{1}$ at the end of the phrase; second, that it is hard to decide between $\hat{3}$ and $\hat{5}$ for the *Kopfton* (is there support for a descent from the latter?)

2 Analyze the passage from mm. 17–32. This reasonably self-contained section is clearly in the relative major of B♭ but finding a unifying thread is again quite tricky. You may want to take careful account of the appoggiatura that appears first in m. 17. The incipit below the main example shows a suggested analysis of the passage from mm. 22–7.

Schenker's analyses

The following six exercises ask you to reconcile Schenker's analyses with the details of the music and consider any particularly interesting issues. You can do most of the basics of these exercises from the examples, but you need to consult the score in order to really understand the context for Schenker's analytical decisions. There is a wealth of analyses from *Free Composition* that can be approached in the same way—these provide a starting point for your explorations.

E1: Beethoven, Sonata Op. 49, No. 2, Tempo di Menuetto, mm. 1–8

Analysis from Schenker 1977: Figure 91/3

Notes: Reconcile Schenker's middleground analysis of the first eight measures of this Menuetto with the score. It is a concise example of how a Schenkerian analysis is an interpretation; explain why Schenker picks these particular notes.

E2: Mozart, Sonata in C major, K. 545, Allegro, exposition

2

Analysis from Schenker 1977: Figure 47/1

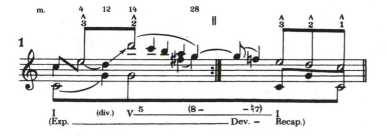

Notes:

1   Look at the opening four measures—why does Schenker show this simply
    as an unfolding?
2   Look at mm. 14–26 and find the fifth progression that Schenker suggests
    prolongs $\hat{2}$ in the exposition
3   Work out what is going on from mm. 5–14. Why does Schenker not
    see this as structurally important?

E3: Beethoven, Sonata in G major, Op. 14, No. 2, Allegro

Analysis from Schenker 1977: Figure 47/2

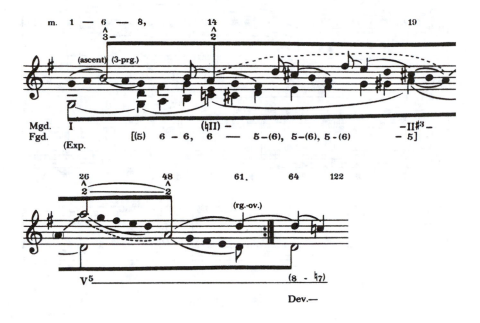

Notes:

1 Reconcile the opening eight measures (a) of the analysis to the score. The first part is fairly easy to reconcile to the analysis but the section from m. 6 is more complicated due to some slightly tricky unfoldings.
2 Find the reaching over figures (marked with eighth-note flags) that Schenker suggests prolong an arpeggiation of A major from mm. 13–20 (b).

E4: Chopin, Mazurka Op. 33, No. 4

Analysis from Schenker 1977: Figure 74/2

Notes: Look at the final passage of this mazurka and work out how Schenker's analysis (from where he writes "end:") relates to the surface of the music. Write a short commentary explaining what this analysis shows (and also what it omits).

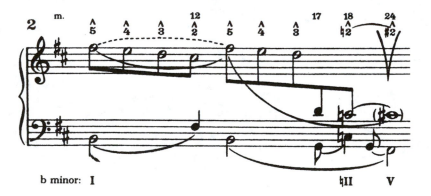

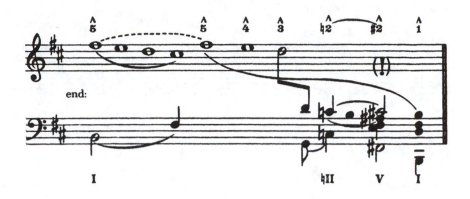

E5: Beethoven, Sonata in A♭ major, Op. 26, Andante con Variazioni

a)

b)

Analysis from Schenker 1977: Figure 85

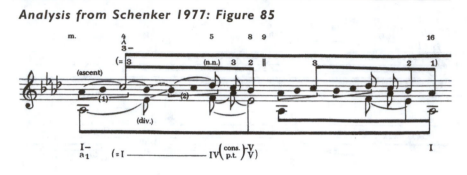

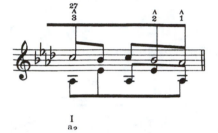

Notes:

1 Reconcile the middleground of the first sixteen measures to Schenker's analysis. Note how structurally important notes that are rhythmically very short can be.

2 What do you think the numbered brackets that Schenker adds to the graph might mean?

3 Look at mm. 26–7, where Beethoven leads back into a reprise of the opening. What is odd about Schenker's interpretation? Explore reasons why one might want to interpret the music in this way?

Glossary

As well as defining key terms and concepts associated with Schenkerian theory, this glossary also indicates where further discussion can be found within the main text. In this book I have used the German terms for the most common Schenkerian concepts (e.g. *Urlinie*, *Ursatz*) but the English terms for others (register transfer rather than *Hoherlegung*). I have nevertheless included most German and English terms in this glossary in order to assist with the reading of other sources. More obscure terms can be found in the index and online glossary.

Anstieg

See **Initial ascent**.

Arpeggiation (Brechung)

An arpeggiation is one of the simplest elaborations, consisting of notes that are consonant with the harmony being prolonged. An arpeggiation is defined as a single movement through notes from one harmony in the same direction. An arpeggiation can only prolong a triad, or a dominant seventh chord. Such chords are treated in more or less the same way as the consonant notes of a triad in much tonal music.

Ausfaltung

See **Unfolding**.

Auskomponierung

Literally translates as "composing out," reflecting Schenker's interest in a process of elaboration from the deep structure of a piece to its surface. The term refers to contrapuntal elaboration of a harmony—the *Ursatz* represents an *Auskomponierung* of the tonic.

Background (Hintergrund)

Strictly speaking, the background refers only to the *Ursatz* form that spans a whole piece or movement. It is used more informally to refer to the *Ursatz* and its immediate prolongations (e.g. initial ascent etc.) that are more properly part of the first level of the middleground.

Bass arpeggiation

See **Bassbrechung**.

Bassbrechung (bass arpeggiation)

Translates literally as "breaking of the bass." The *Bassbrechung* is the I–V–I that underpins the *Urlinie* as part of the *Ursatz*, including any elaborations of this pattern. Typical elaborations are I–III–V–I and I–II–V–I.

Brechung

See **Arpeggiation**.

Cadential six-four (6/4)

A cadential six-four is a double appoggiatura onto the dominant chord—the numbers refer to the figured bass pattern of a sixth and a fourth over the root of the dominant falling to a fifth and third. Some traditional systems of harmonic analysis label the cadential six-four as a second inversion tonic chord—this is not exactly wrong, but it is a less accurate description of its function.

Composing out

See **Auskomponierung**.

Consonant skip

A consonant skip is a term invented by Allen Forte and used by some Schenkerians to refer to simple two-note arpeggiations, which usually constitute some sort of unfolding.

Coupling (Koppelung)

A coupling is a change of register within one voice that connects two pitches one or more octaves apart. In relation to the *Ursatz* it is subtly different from a register transfer. While the latter simply transfers a note of the *Urlinie* (or one of its elaborations) into a different octave, a coupling involves several such changes of octave, which combine to create a long-term connection between the two registers. A coupling, therefore, is made up of a number of register transfers.

Diminution

A term used by Schenker to describe the embellishment of simpler musical structures beneath the surface of the music. The process of analysis is partly one of looking "behind" the surface diminutions, but Schenker was more interested in a process of generation from background to foreground.

Dividing dominant (Oberquint-Teiler)

Dividing dominant is the term for the structural chord V that underpins the first $\hat{2}$ of an interrupted *Urlinie*. The term is also used to refer to dominant chords that perform a similar function in the middleground.

Fifth progression or 5-prg (Quintzug or 5-zug)

See **Linear progression**.

First level middleground

This term refers to the immediate prolongations of the *Ursatz*. Schenker restricts such prolongations to a small number of strictly defined forms. Elaborations at this level of the structure are often informally referred to as the background.

Foreground (Vordergrund)

Schenker conceives of music in terms of layers of elaboration from the "deep" structure to the surface. A foreground analysis is concerned with the surface of the music.

Fourth progression or 4-prg (Quartzug or 4-zug)

See **Linear progression**.

Fundamental descent

See *Urlinie*.

Fundamental structure

See *Ursatz*.

Harmonic unit

The term harmonic unit is used in this book to refer to a harmonic progression that is grouped together in the process of analysis. The most common harmonic units are I–V–I, I–V and V–I, which can be elaborated by other chords (e.g. I–VI–II–V–I). Harmonic units are linked with melodic elaborations into "linear-harmonic units" in the process of layer analysis. A third progression, for example, might be said to elaborate the harmonic unit of I–V–I.

Hoherlegung

See **Register transfer**.

Initial ascent (Anstieg)

An initial ascent is a rising linear progression to the primary tone (or *Kopfton*) of the *Urlinie* (i.e. $\hat{3}$ or $\hat{5}$) and, as a very deep level elaboration of the *Ursatz*, might span many bars. The initial ascent is one of the most common constituents of the first level of the middleground.

Interruption (Unterbrechung)

This is an elaboration of the *Ursatz* in which the *Urlinie* descends to $\hat{2}/V$, returns to the *Kopfton* and begins the descent to $\hat{1}$ again. An interrupted *Urlinie* from $\hat{3}$ would thus read as follows: $\hat{3}\ \hat{2}\ |\ |\ \hat{3}\ \hat{2}\ \hat{1}$. Note the double vertical line that is used to indicate the point of interruption. This is one the most important *Ursatz* elaborations because it creates a structural division on the dominant at the point of interruption ($\hat{2}/V$) that frequently corresponds to the end of the A section of binary (and indeed sonata) form pieces. In orthodox Schenkerian theory the interruption after $\hat{2}$ is the only possible division of the *Urlinie*.

Kopfton (primary tone or head tone)

The *Kopfton* is the first note of the *Urlinie* (i.e. $\hat{3}$, $\hat{5}$ or $\hat{8}$). Decisions about whether the *Kopfton* is $\hat{3}$ or $\hat{5}$ can make a considerable difference to the rest of an analysis. If the *Urlinie* is elaborated by, for example, an initial ascent, the *Kopfton* will not be right at the beginning of the piece.

Koppelung

See **Coupling**.

Layer or level (Schicht)

The idea that music consists of a series of layers of elaboration is fundamental to Schenkerian theory. Many scholars translate Schenker's term *Schicht* as "level" but "layer" is probably closer to the sense in which it is used. Schenkerian analysts refer to a graph as a depiction of a particular layer of the structure, although it is rare for a graph to show only one layer of elaborations.

Leerlauf

See **Unsupported stretch**.

Linear progression (Zug)

A linear progression is the Schenkerian term for a passing note elaboration. A linear progression elaborates a specific harmony in the middleground or foreground. Its first and last notes must make sense of the harmony at the goal of the progression. A linear progression moves in only one direction and can thus be classified either as ascending or descending.

Schenker understands a linear progression as the unfolding of a two-note interval made up of its initial and final note—it is the interval between these notes that gives a linear progression its name. The names of the most common linear progressions and their abbreviations are given below:

- third progression (spanning a third)—3-prg
- fourth progression (spanning a fourth)—4-prg
- fifth progression (spanning a fifth)—5-prg
- sixth progression (spanning a sixth)—6-prg
- octave progression (spanning an octave)—8-prg

Middleground (Mittelgrund)

The foreground is the surface layer of a piece of music, and the background is the deepest layer, of which the whole piece is understood to be an elaboration. The middleground is the variable number of layers that a Schenkerian analysis will identify in between the foreground and background.

Mischung

See **Mixture**.

Mittelgrund

See **Middleground**.

Mixture (Mischung)

Schenker most often uses the term mixture to refer to alternation between major and minor thirds. Mixture is a common feature of the first level middleground and is easiest to illustrate by way of an example. Imagine that a minuet in A major is interpreted as a descent from $\hat{3}$ and that the trio section is in A minor. The overall shape of such a minuet might be as follows:

$\sharp\hat{3}$ (Minuet) $\natural\hat{3}$ (Trio) $\sharp\hat{3}$ (repeat of Minuet)

This alternation of minor and major $\hat{3}$ is called mixture.

Motion from inner voice (Untergreifen)

Schenker uses this term to refer to a linear progression that ascends to a note of the *Urlinie*. Because a linear progression is understood as the unfolding of a two-note chord outlined by its first and last notes, an ascending linear progression is said to move from the lower (or inner) voice of this chord to the upper voice. In the first level middleground, Schenker suggests that linear progressions can only ascend to or descend from notes of the *Urlinie*. A motion from the inner voice to the *Kopfton* is usually referred to as an initial ascent.

Nebennote

See **Neighbor note**.

Neighbor note (Nebennote)

A neighbor note elaborates a note of a chord through stepwise motion to and/or from a dissonance. A complete neighbor note moves stepwise to a dissonance and back again. An incomplete neighbor note can either move from the dissonance to the consonance or the reverse.

Oberquint-Teiler

See **Dividing dominant**.

Obligate Lage

See **Obligatory register**.

Obligatory register (Obligate Lage)

Schenker suggests that, if a piece starts in a given register, we expect it also to conclude in that same register. The principle ultimately relates to the *Urlinie* in that a Schenkerian analyst will usually expect to find the final descent to $\hat{1}$ in the same octave that was established by the *Kopfton*.

Primary tone (Kopfton)

See *Kopfton*.

Prolongation

Prolongation refers to the elaboration of contrapuntal structures. All tonal pieces are therefore, in Schenkerian terms, a prolongation of the *Ursatz*.

Reaching over (Uebergrifen)

The concept of reaching over depends on Schenker's understanding of tonal music as being made up of different voices. If a melodic line leaps upwards and then falls by step to the next main note of the melody, it is said to be "reaching over" the principal voice.

Register transfer (Hoherlegung (up) Teiferlegung (down))

A register transfer simply means a change of octave. It is important, however, in describing the relationship of surface embellishments to the underlying simpler progressions that they prolong. A middleground descending third progression, for example, might be elaborated in the foreground by one or more of its notes being transferred up or down an octave. Register transfers are often found in relation to the notes of the *Urlinie*. Go to the definition of coupling to see how a coupling subtly differs from a register transfer.

Scale degree

Numbered degrees of the scale from $\hat{1}$ to $\hat{8}$. Such caretted numbers refer back to the scale of the main key unless otherwise stated. Usually, scale degree labels are reserved for notes of the *Urlinie*.

Scale step (Stufe)

Schenker uses the term scale step to refer to the principal steps of the *Bassbrechung* (the bass part of the *Ursatz*). If the *Bassbrechung* basically outlines the progression I–III–V–I then these chords would be considered scale steps whereas, for example, a secondary dominant onto III would not. The term thus distinguishes between diatonic structural harmonies and chords that are understood as embellishments of those harmonies.

Schicht

See Layer or level.

Six-four chord

See Cadential six-four.

Stufe

See Scale step.

Teiferlegung

See Register transfer.

Terztieler

See Third divider.

Third divider (Terztieler)

Schenker uses this term to refer to the elaboration of the *Bassbrechung* through III, with the resulting bass progression of I–III–V–I. The third divider is particularly important in minor keys, in which there is often considerable prolongation of III as the relative major.

Third progression

See Linear progression.

Tonicization

Tonicization is the Schenkerian term for what is traditionally called modulation. If a piece modulates from the tonic to the dominant, Schenker refers to this as a tonicization of V. The use of this term emphasizes the fact that a tonal piece is ultimately understood as a contrapuntal realization of the tonic.

Uebergrifen

See Reaching over.

Unfolding (Ausfaltung)

A unfolding literally unfolds a two-note chord, moving from either from upper voice to lower or the other way round. Unfoldings are often found in conjunction with other types of elaboration, such as linear progressions.

Unsupported stretch (Leerlauf)

In an *Urlinie* that descends from $\hat{5}$, the $\hat{4}$ is theoretically dissonant with the I over which it appears in the background. Schenker thus calls the background motion from $\hat{5}$ to $\hat{3}$ the "unsupported stretch," because there is no harmonic support for the $\hat{4}$. One of the criteria for deciding whether a piece is a descent from $\hat{5}$ is whether this theoretically dissonant $\hat{4}$ receives harmonic support in the middleground and foreground. If there is no harmonic support for $\hat{4}$ and it therefore remains dissonant in the foreground, then the piece is more likely to be a descent from $\hat{3}$. A descent from $\hat{8}$ obviously has a much more complicated unsupported stretch, which is why it is so rare.

Unterbrechung

See **Interruption**.

Untergreifen

See **Motion from inner voice**.

Urlinie (fundamental descent)

The *Urlinie* is the top line of the two-part *Ursatz*, comprising a stepwise descent from $\hat{3}$, $\hat{5}$ or $\hat{8}$ to $\hat{1}$. The term is usually translated as "fundamental descent," reflecting Schenker's belief that this archetypal descending motion underpins all tonal pieces.

Ursatz (fundamental structure)

The *Ursatz* is the archetypal progression of which all tonal pieces are hypothetically an elaboration. It consists of descending line in the upper part (*Urlinie*) over a bass progression (*Bassbrechung*). It is discussed in detail in Chapter 4.

Voice exchange (Stimmentausch)

A voice exchange is where two voices exchange notes from the same chord. An example would be where a top voice moved from E down to C while a lower voice moved from C up to E an octave lower. In this circumstance the two voices have literally exchanged notes from the chord of C major. A voice exchange involves simultaneous unfoldings in two different voices.

Vordergrund

See **Foreground**.

Zug

See **Linear progression**.

Notes

1 Introduction

1 Schenker 1977: 6.

2 An overview of the basics

1 I follow the common practice of Schenkerian analysts in employing a mixture of Schenker's original German terms and their standard translations to refer to the key concepts. Where the English is particularly awkward or the German is in very common usage, I have employed Schenker's original terms. In the interest of consistency I have given the German equivalents of most terms, even if I do not use them in the text.

2 Forte and Gilbert 1982.

3 Cadwallader and Gagné 1998: 86.

3 Larger-scale structures

1 Taking their cue from a famous attack on the prevailing analytical and musicological orthodoxies by Joseph Kerman, a number of prominent scholars, including Kofi Agawu, Jonathan Kramer and Kevin Korsyn, have developed approaches that shift the analytical focus away from unity. Other scholars have, in turn, defended unity as an analytical paradigm, notably Robert P. Morgan in Volume 22, Nos. 1-2 of *Music Analysis* (Morgan 2003). His article is treated to a lengthy multi-authored rebuttal in Volume 23, Nos. 2-3.

2 See Schenker 1954: 217.

3 If you include those chorales that end on a non-tonic chord with the root in the soprano voice, only 12 out of 371 do not end on $\hat{1}$.

4 This does not include movements that *segue attacca* into the next, such as the second movement of Op. 27, No. 1. Schenker would locate the structural ending of many of these movements before the beginning of the coda so, from his point of view, far fewer than this genuinely end on scale degrees other than $\hat{1}$.

5 The exceptions are Fugues 2 and 23 from the first book and 3 and 15 from the second.

6 Schenker 1977: 107.

7 An ascending register transfer is *Hoherlegung* and a descending one is *Teiferlegung*. In Anglo-American scholarship, these terms are invariably rendered in their English translations.

5 Presenting a Schenkerian analysis

1   The notation of these bass patterns follows the convention established in Schenker 1977: Figures 15–19.
2   For an interesting discussion of the relationship between traditional and Schenkerian form see Smith 1996: 191–297.
3   Salzer 1982.

6 Schenkerian analysis and form

1   Schenker 1977: 5.
2   Schenker 1977: 129.
3   Schenker 1977: 133.
4   Rosen 1988: 6.
5   Rosen 1988: 12.
6   In fact, Schenker explicitly rules out other *Ursatz* elaborations. See Schenker 1977: 134.
7   In minor key sonata forms the second subject is in a major key in the exposition; when this is transposed into the tonic in the recapitulation, composers have additionally to decide whether to keep this material in the major or alter it so that it is recapitulated in the tonic minor.
8   Schenker 1977: 138.

7 Playing with register

1   Translated in *The Masterwork in Music* (Schenker 1994).
2   Schenker 1977: 6.
3   Schenker 1977: 6.
4   For Schenker's view on music and genius see Schenker 1977: xxii–xxiv.
5   The tone and content of some of *Der Tonwille* makes clear the extent to which Schenker's view of culture goes hand in hand with a wider dislike for the non-German world, although this is to some extent explained by the general bitterness about the Treaty of Versailles prevalent in the years after the First World War.
6   Schenker 1977: 5.
7   Schenker 1977: 5.
8   Schenker 2004: 60.

8 Parallelisms and dramatic structure

1   Schenker 1954: 6.
2   Schenker 1977: 99.
3   Schenker 2004: 25 ff.
4   Schenker interprets the e♭1 as a 6-5 motion onto d1 and thus the harmony of the first four measures is simply an elaboration of the dominant. By marking the d1 as a neighbor note to e♭1 my analysis implies that the tonic is the principal harmony. Although Schenker's 6-5 interpretation makes good musical sense, the logic of my analysis is simpler and would be the more likely outcome of approaching the passage according to the methods outlined in previous chapters.
5   Schenker 2004: 27.
6   Schenker calls this series of descending motions the *Urlinie* but they do not correspond to his later conception of the *Urlinie* as a single descending line across the whole movement.
7   Schenker 2004: 145.

9 Beyond Schenker

1   The remaining 10 percent of musical examples are taken from a smattering of major and minor figures from around the same time period. The only exceptions are Josquin and Hugo Wolf, who each contribute a single example.
2   See Brian Hyer's article, 'Tonality' (Hyer n.d.), for a succinct overview of the metaphorical descriptions of the tonal system employed by Riepel and other tonal theorists.
3   See Damschroeder and Williams 1990.
4   See, for example, *Counterpoint Vol. I* (Schenker 2001: xxii); see also the sideswipes at Bruckner in Schenker 2004: 77 and Schenker 1977: 89.
5   See Schenker 1954: 188 ff. and Schenker 1977: 63.
6   Kramer 1981: 191–208.
7   Schenker 1977: 89.
8   Schenker 1977: 131.
9   Benjamin 1983: 28–50.

Group A—Foreground analysis

1   Some of these exercises have been slightly changed from the original music in order to make a neater start or end to the extract.

Select bibliography

This bibliography lists only those sources on Schenkerian analysis mentioned directly in the text. The existence of two comprehensive and up-to-date research guides—Ayotte (2004) and Berry (2004)—makes a full bibliography redundant. There is also a longer bibliography available at www.SchenkerGUIDE.com.

Ayotte, Benjamin (2004) *Heinrich Schenker: A Guide to Research*, New York: Routledge.

Benjamin, William (1983) "Models of Underlying Tonal Structure: How Can They be Abstract, and How Should They be Abstract," *Music Theory Spectrum* 5: 28–50.

Berry, David (2004) *A Topical Guide to Schenkerian Literature*, Hillsdale NY: Pendragon Press.

Cadwallader, Allen and David Gagné (1998) *Analysis of Tonal Music: A Schenkerian Approach*, Oxford: Oxford University Press.

Cook, Nicholas (1994) *A Guide to Musical Analysis*, Oxford: Oxford University Press.

—— (1999) "Heinrich Schenker, Modernist: Detail, Difference and Analysis," *Theory and Practice* 24: 91–106.

Damschroeder, David and David Williams (1990) *Music Theory from Zarlino to Schenker: A Bibliography and Guide*, New York: Pendragon Press.

Forte, Allen (1984) "Middleground Motives in the Adagietto of Mahler's Fifth Symphony," *Nineteenth-Century Music* 8: 153–63.

—— and Stephen Gilbert (1982) *Introduction to Schenkerian Analysis*, New York: Norton.

Hyer, Brian (n.d.) "Tonality," *Grove Music Online* (at www.grovemusic.com).

Jonas, Oswald (1982) *Introduction to the Theory of Heinrich Schenker: the Nature of the Musical Work of Art*, New York: Longman.

Kramer, Lawrence (1981) "The Mirror of Tonality: Transitional Features of Nineteenth-Century Harmony," *19th-Century Music*, 4: 191–208.

Morgan, Robert P. (2003) "The Concept of Unity and Musical Analysis," *Music Analysis*, 22/1–2: 7–50.

Rosen, Charles (1988) *Sonata Forms*, rev. ed., New York: Norton.

Salzer, Felix (1982) *Structural Hearing*, New York: Dover Publications.

Schachter, Carl (1999) *Unfoldings: Essays in Schenkerian Theory and Analysis*, ed. Joseph Straus. Oxford: Oxford University Press.

Schenker, Heinrich (1954) *Harmony*, ed. Oswald Jonas, tr. Elizabeth Mann Borgese, Cambridge MA: MIT.

—— (1969) *Five Graphic Analyses*, New York: Dover.

—— (1977) *Free Composition*, ed. Oswald Jonas tr. Ernst Oster, New York: Pendragon.

—— (1994) *The Masterwork in Music: Volume I*, tr. & ed. William Drabkin, tr. I. Bent, R. Kramer, J. Rothgeb and H. Siegel, Cambridge: Cambridge University Press.

—— (1996a) *The Masterwork in Music: Volume II*, tr. & ed. William Drabkin and Ian Bent, tr. John Rothgeb and Hedi Siegel, Cambridge: Cambridge University Press.

—— (1996b) *The Masterwork in Music: Volume III*, tr. & ed. William Drabkin, tr. Ian Bent, Alfred Clayton and Derrick Puffett, Cambridge: Cambridge University Press.

—— (2001) *Counterpoint Vol. I*, ed. & tr. John Rothgeb, tr. Jurgen Thym, New York: Schirmer.

—— (2004) *Der Tonwille: Pamphlets in Witness of the Immutable Laws of Music: Volume I*, tr. & ed. William Drabkin, tr. Ian Ben, Joseph Dubiel, Timothy Jackson, Joseph Lubben and Robert Snarrenburg, Oxford: Oxford University Press.

Smith, Charles (1996) "Musical Form and Fundamental Structure: An Investigation of Schenker's *Formenlehre*," *Music Analysis* 15/2–3: 191–297.

Snarrenberg, Robert (1994) "Competing Myths: The American Abandonment of Schenker's Organicism," in *Theory, Analysis and Meaning in Music*, ed. Anthony Pople, Cambridge: Cambridge University Press.

Index